500 FACTS
Animals

First published in 2009 by Miles Kelly Publishing Ltd
Bardfield Centre, Great Bardfield, Essex, CM7 4SL

Copyright © Miles Kelly Publishing Ltd 2009

The sections in this book are also available as individual titles

2 4 6 8 10 9 7 5 3 1

Editorial Director Belinda Gallagher
Art Director Jo Brewer
Editions Manager Bethan Ellish
Cover Designer Simon Lee
Designers Angela Ashton, Joe Jones, Sally Lace, Elaine Wilkinson
Editor Rosie McGuire
Indexer Jane Parker
Production Manager Elizabeth Brunwin
Reprographics Stephan Davis, Jennifer Hunt, Ian Paulyn
Contributors Trevor Day, Dr Jim Flegg,
Jinny Johnson, Ann Kay, Steve Parker

ISBN 978-1-84810-199-9

Printed in China

British Library Cataloguing-in-Publication Data
A catalogue record for this book is available from the British Library

ACKNOWLEDGEMENTS
The publishers would like to thank the following
sources for the use of their photographs:

Corbis 86/87 Michael Prince; 90/91 Amos Nachoum
FLPA 76 Fred Bavendam/Minden Pictures
Pictorial Press 89 Warner Bros

All other photographs are from:
Corel, digitalSTOCK, digitalvision, Fotolia.com, iStockphoto.com,
John Foxx, PhotoAlto, PhotoDisc, PhotoEssentials, PhotoPro, Stockbyte

All artworks from the Miles Kelly Artwork Bank

Made with paper from a sustainable forest

www.mileskelly.net
info@mileskelly.net

www.factsforprojects.com
The one-stop homework helper – pictures, facts, videos, projects and more

Contents

MAMMALS 176-217

1 **Insects are among the most numerous and widespread animals on Earth.** They form the largest of all animal groups, with millions of different kinds, or species, that live almost everywhere in the world. But not all creepy-crawlies are insects. Spiders belong to a different group called arachnids, and millipedes are in yet another group!

Tiger swallowtail butterfly

Spiny green nymph

Crickets

Stick insects

Tarantula

Dragonfly

Cockchafer
beetle

Stag beetles

Honeybees

Millipede

Giant longhorn
beetle

Wood ants

Tarantula
hawk wasp

Insects everywhere!

2 **The housefly is one of the most common, widespread and annoying insects.** There are many other members of the fly group, such as bluebottles, horseflies, craneflies ('daddy longlegs') and fruitflies. They all have two wings. Most other kinds of insects have four wings.

Housefly

3 **The ladybird is a noticeable insect with its bright red or yellow body and black spots.** It is a member of the beetle group. This is the biggest of all insect groups, with more than half a million kinds, from massive goliath and rhinoceros beetles to tiny flea-beetles and weevil-beetles.

Ladybird

4 **The white butterfly is not usually welcome in the garden.** Their young, known as caterpillars, eat the leaves of the gardener's precious flowers and vegetables. There are thousands of kinds of butterflies and even more kinds of their night-time cousins, the moths.

▼ Insects like these white butterflies do not have a bony skeleton inside their bodies like we do. Their bodies are covered by a series of horny plates. This is called an exoskeleton.

White butterfly feeding from a flower

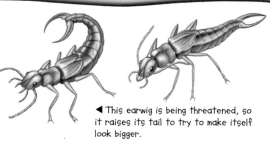

5 The earwig is a familiar insect in the park, garden, garage, shed — and sometimes house. Despite their name, earwigs do not crawl into ears or hide in wigs. But they do like dark, damp corners. Earwigs form one of the smaller insect groups, with only 1300 different kinds.

◄ This earwig is being threatened, so it raises its tail to try to make itself look bigger.

▲ Ants use their antennae and sense of touch as a means of communication.

SPOT THE INSECTS!

Have you seen any insects so far today? Maybe a fly whizzing around the house or a butterfly flitting among the flowers? On a warm summer's day you probably see many kinds of insects. On a cold winter's day there are fewer insects about. Most are hiding away or have not yet hatched out of their eggs.

6 Ants are fine in the garden or wood, but are pests in the house. Ants, bees and wasps make up a large insect group with some 300,000 different kinds. Most can sting, although many are too small to hurt people. However, some, such as bulldog ants, have a painful bite.

7 The scorpionfly has a nasty looking sting on a long curved tail. It flies or crawls in bushes and weeds during summer. Only the male scorpionfly has the red tail. It looks like the sting of a scorpion but is harmless.

How insects grow

8 **All insects begin life inside an egg.** The female insect usually lays her eggs in an out-of-the-way place, such as under a stone, leaf or bark, or in the soil.

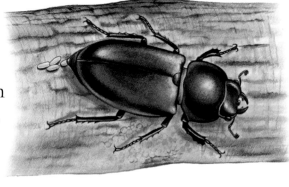

▲ The female stag beetle lays her eggs in rotting wood. Larvae hatch and feed on wood for up to six years before they pupate.

9 **When some types of insects hatch, they do not look like their parents.** A young beetle, butterfly or fly is very different from a grown-up beetle, butterfly or fly. It is soft-bodied, wriggly and worm-like. This young stage is called a larva. There are different names for various kinds of larvae. A fly larva is called a maggot, a beetle larva is a grub and a butterfly larva is a caterpillar.

10 **A female insect mates with a male insect before she can lay her eggs.** The female and male come together to check that they are both the same kind of insect, and they are both healthy and ready to mate. This is known as courtship. Butterflies often flit through the air together in a 'courtship dance'.

◀ Large caterpillars always eat into the centre of the leaf from the edge. Caterpillars grasp the leaf with their legs, while their specially developed front jaws chew at their food.

◄ This butterfly is emerging from its pupal case and is stretching its wings for the first time.

13 Some kinds of insects change shape less as they grow up. When a young cricket or grasshopper hatches from its egg, it looks similar to its parents. However it may not have any wings yet.

11 The larva eats and eats. It sheds its skin several times so it can grow. Then it changes into the next stage of its life, called a pupa. The pupa has a hard outer case which stays still and inactive. But, inside, the larva is changing body shape again. This change of shape is known as metamorphosis.

12 At last the pupa's case splits open and the adult insect crawls out. Its body, legs and wings spread out and harden. Now the insect is ready to find food and also find a mate.

14 The young cricket eats and eats, and sheds or moults its skin several times as it grows. Each time it looks more like its parent. A young insect which resembles the fully grown adult like this is called a nymph. At the last moult it becomes a fully formed adult, ready to feed and breed.

I DON'T BELIEVE IT!

Courtship is a dangerous time for the male praying mantis. The female is much bigger than the male, and as soon as they have mated, she may eat him!

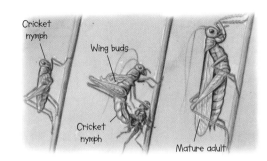

Cricket nymph

Wing buds

Cricket nymph

Mature adult

Air aces

15 **Most kinds of insects have two pairs of wings and use them to fly from place to place.** One of the strongest fliers is the Apollo butterfly of Europe and Asia. It flaps high over hills and mountains, then rests on a rock or flower in the sunshine.

Apollo butterfly

17 **Some insects flash bright lights as they fly.** The firefly is not a fly but a type of beetle. Male fireflies 'dance' in the air at dusk, the rear parts of their bodies glowing on and off about once each second. Female fireflies stay on twigs and leaves and glow in reply as part of their courtship.

16 **A fast and fierce flying hunter is the dragonfly.** Its huge eyes spot tiny prey such as midges and mayflies. The dragonfly dashes through the air, turns in a flash, grabs the victim in its legs and whirrs back to a perch to eat its meal.

18

The smallest fliers include gnats, midges and mosquitoes. These are all true flies, with one pair of wings. Some are almost too tiny for us to see. Certain types bite animals and people, sucking their blood as food.

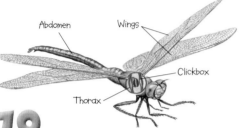

Abdomen

Wings

Clickbox

Thorax

19

An insect's wings are attached to the middle part of its body, the thorax. This is like a box with strong walls, called a clickbox. Muscles inside the thorax pull to make the walls click in and out, which makes the wings flick up and down. A large butterfly flaps its wings once or twice each second. Some tiny flies flap almost 1000 times each second.

MAKE A FLAPPING FLY

You will need:

stiff card   tissue paper
round-ended scissors   sticky tape

1. Ask an adult for help. Carefully cut out the card to make a box with two open ends as shown.

2. Use strips of stiff card to make struts for the wings and attach these to the side walls of the box. Make the rest of the wings from tissue paper.

3. Hold the box as shown. Move the top and bottom walls in, then out. This bends the side walls and makes the wings flap, just like a real insect.

20

A few insects lack wings. They are mostly very small and live in the soil, such as bristletails and springtails. One kind of bristletail is the silverfish – a small, shiny, fast-running insect.

Champion leapers

21 **Many insects move around mainly by hopping and jumping, rather than flying.** They have long, strong legs and can leap great distances, especially to avoid enemies and escape from danger. Grasshoppers are up to 15 centimetres long. Most have very long back legs and some types can jump more than 3 metres. Often the grasshopper opens its brightly patterned wings briefly as it leaps, giving a flash of colour.

22 **The champion leaping insects, for their body size, are fleas.** They are mostly small, just 2–3 millimetres long. But they can jump over 30 centimetres, which is more than 100 times their body size. Fleas suck blood or body fluids from warm-blooded animals, mainly mammals but also birds.

Grasshopper

23 An insect leaper that jumps with its tail, rather than its legs, is the springtail. Springtails are tiny, 1–3 millimetres long, or as long as this letter 'l'! Some types can leap more than 5 centimetres.

24 The click beetle, or skipjack, is another insect leaper. This beetle is about 12 millimetres long. When in danger it falls on its back and pretends to be dead. But it slowly arches its body and then straightens with a jerk and a 'click'. It can flick itself about 25 centimetres into the air!

QUIZ

Which type of insect can jump farthest?

Put these insects in order of how far they can leap.
Grasshopper   Flea
Click beetle   Springtail

Now put them in order of how far they can leap compared to their sizes.

Answers:
The grasshopper can jump farthest, then the flea, click beetle and finally the springtail. The flea can jump farthest for its size, then the click beetle, the springtail and finally the grasshopper.

Click beetle

Springtail

▲ The 'tail' rear part of the springtail's body, is shaped like a V or Y. It is usually folded under the body and held in place by a trigger-like flap. When the flap moves aside the 'tail' flicks down and flips the insect through the air.

Super sprinters

25 **Some insects rarely fly or leap.** They prefer to run, and run, and run… all day, and even all night too. Among the champion insect runners are cockroaches. They are tough and adaptable, with about 3600 different kinds. A few burrow in soil or live in caves. But most scurry speedily across the ground on their long legs. They have low, flat bodies and can dart into narrow crevices, under logs and stones and bricks, and into cupboards, furniture – and beds!

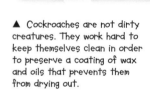

▲ Cockroaches are not dirty creatures. They work hard to keep themselves clean in order to preserve a coating of wax and oils that prevents them from drying out.

▼ Tiger beetles have huge eyes. They use their massive biting jaws to catch and cut up their food.

26 **The green tiger beetle is an active hunter that races over open ground almost too fast for our eyes to follow.** It chases smaller creatures such as ants, woodlice, worms and little spiders. It has huge jaws for its size and soon rips apart any victim.

27 One of the busiest insect walkers is the devil's coach-horse, a type of beetle with a long body that resembles an earwig. It belongs to the group known as rove beetles which walk huge distances to find food. The devil's coach-horse has powerful mouthparts and tears apart dead and dying small caterpillars, grubs and worms.

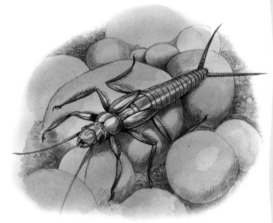

▲ The stonefly nymph, the larva of the stonefly, runs around on the bed of its river home searching for food.

Devil's coach-horse

28 Some insects walk not only across the ground, but also up smooth, shiny surfaces such as walls and even windows. They have wide feet with many tiny hooks or sticky pads. These grip bumps that are too small to see in substances such as glossy, wet leaves or window glass.

Stunning swimmers

29 **Many kinds of insects live underwater in ponds, streams, rivers and lakes.** Some walk about on the bottom, such as the young forms or nymphs of dragonflies and damselflies. Others swim strongly using their legs as oars to row through the water. The great diving beetle hunts small water creatures such as tadpoles and baby fish. It can give a person a painful bite in self-defence.

30 Some water insects, such as the great silver water beetle, breathe air. So they must come to the surface for fresh supplies. The hairs on the beetle's body trap tiny bubbles of air for breathing below.

Mayfly nymphs

Damselfly nymph

31
Some insects even walk on water. The pond skater has a slim, light body with long, wide-splayed legs. It glides across the surface 'skin' or film caused by the feature of water known as surface tension. It is a member of the bug group of insects and eats tiny animals that fall into the pond.

32
The nymphs of dragonflies, damselflies, stoneflies and mayflies have tails with feathery gills. These work like the gills of a fish, for breathing underwater. These young insects never need to go to the surface until they change into adults.

Pond skater

MAKE AN INSECT DIVING SUIT

Young caddisflies, called nymphs, make tube-shaped cases, called caddis cases. These protect the nymph's body underwater. They are made using small bits which the nymph collects from its surroundings. Each caddis uses different bits to make its case. You can make your own caddis case, and you can even choose what sort of caddis you want to be!

With the help of an adult, roll up some pieces of cardboard to make tubes to wear on your forearm. Stick bits on to build giant caddis cases. Make:
a great red sedge caddis of leaves or
a silver-horn caddis of pebbles
and pieces of grit
Put your arm through a tube
and wiggle your fingers like
the caddis's head!

Great diving beetle

Dragonfly nymph

Brilliant burrowers

33 Soil teems with millions of creatures — and many are insects. Some are the worm-like young forms of insects, called larvae or grubs, as shown below. Others are fully grown insects, such as burrowing beetles, ants, termites, springtails and earwigs. These soil insects are a vital source of food for all kinds of larger animals from spiders and shrews to moles and many types of birds.

35 The larva of the click beetle is shiny orange, up to 25 millimetres long and called a wireworm. It stays undergound, feeding on plant parts, for up to five years. Then it changes into an adult and leaves the soil. Wireworms can be serious pests of cereal crops such as barley, oats and wheat. They also eat beet and potatoes that you would find underground.

◀ The European mole burrows and feeds on the insects and worms that live in the soil.

Cranefly

Cranefly larva, leatherjacket

34 However, insects in the soil can also cause great damage to plants, especially farm crops. They eat roots and other underground parts, especially crops such as potatoes and carrots.

▶ Many insects pose a threat to farmers' crops. Farmers can use pesticides, chemicals to kill the insects, but many people think that this harms other plants and animals.

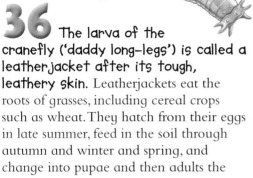

36 The larva of the cranefly ('daddy long-legs') is called a leatherjacket after its tough, leathery skin. Leatherjackets eat the roots of grasses, including cereal crops such as wheat. They hatch from their eggs in late summer, feed in the soil through autumn and winter and spring, and change into pupae and then adults the next summer.

QUIZ

Sort out the following items into three groups:

A Larger animals which eat insect larvae
B Insect larvae
C Plants eaten by larvae

1. Crow
2. Potato
3. Wireworm
4. Mole
5. Cicada grub
6. Carrot

Answers:
A.1 and 4. B.3 and 5.
C.2 and 6.

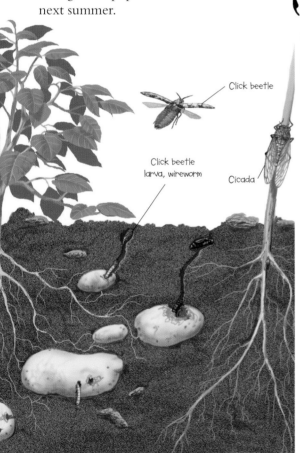

Click beetle

Click beetle larva, wireworm

Cicada

37 The larva of the cicada may live underground for more than ten years. Different types of cicadas stay in the soil for different periods of time. The American periodic cicada is probably the record-holder, taking 17 years to change into a pupa and then an adult. Cicada larvae suck juices from plant roots. Grown-up cicadas make loud chirping or buzzing sounds.

Cicada larva

Bloodthirsty bugs

38 Most insects may be small, but they are among the fiercest and hungriest hunters in the animal world. Many have mouthparts shaped like spears or saws, which are relatively big compared to their bodies, for grabbing and tearing up victims. Some actively chase after prey. Others lie in wait and surprise the prey.

Antenna detects smells

Jaws used for digging and cutting up food

Wasp's head

39 The lacewing looks delicate and dainty as it sits on a leaf by day or flies gently at night. However, it is a fearsome hunter of smaller creatures, especially aphids such as greenfly and blackfly. It chews the aphid and drinks its body fluids. It may also have a sip of sweet, sugary nectar from a flower.

Lacewing eating an aphid

40 One of the most powerful insect predators is the praying mantis. It is called the praying mantis since it holds its front legs folded, like a person with hands together in prayer. But the front legs have sharp spines and snap together like spiky scissors to grab caterpillars, moths and similar food.

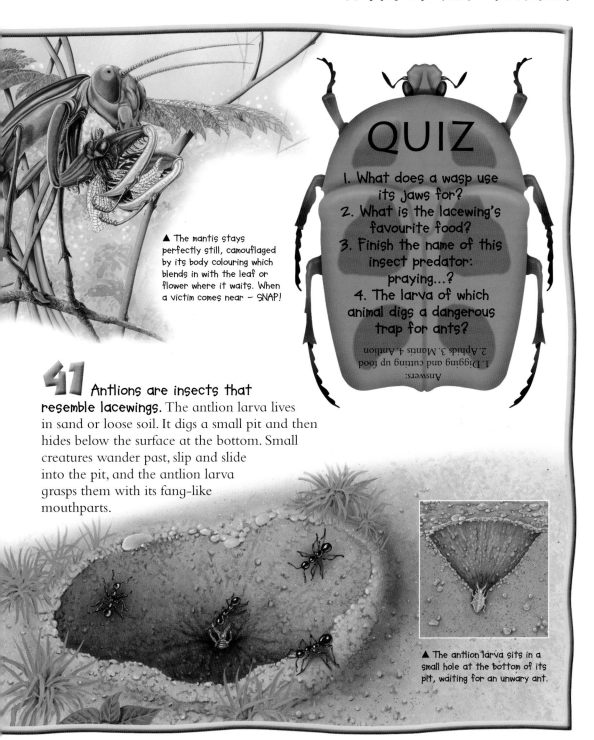

▲ The mantis stays perfectly still, camouflaged by its body colouring which blends in with the leaf or flower where it waits. When a victim comes near — SNAP!

QUIZ

1. What does a wasp use its jaws for?
2. What is the lacewing's favourite food?
3. Finish the name of this insect predator: praying...?
4. The larva of which animal digs a dangerous trap for ants?

Answers:
1. Digging and cutting up food 2. Aphids 3. Mantis 4. Antlion

41 **Antlions are insects that resemble lacewings.** The antlion larva lives in sand or loose soil. It digs a small pit and then hides below the surface at the bottom. Small creatures wander past, slip and slide into the pit, and the antlion larva grasps them with its fang-like mouthparts.

▲ The antlion larva sits in a small hole at the bottom of its pit, waiting for an unwary ant.

25

Veggie bugs

42 About nine out of ten kinds of insects eat some kind of plant food. Many feed on soft, rich, nutritious substances. These include the sap in stems and leaves, the mineral-rich liquid in roots, the nectar in flowers and the soft flesh of squashy fruits and berries.

43 Solid wood may not seem very tasty, but many kinds of insects eat it. They usually consume the wood when they are larvae or grubs, making tunnels as they eat their way through trees, logs, and timber structures such as bridges, fences, houses and furniture.

Elm beetle

Elm beetle larva

Furniture beetle

Flowerbug

Mealy-bug

Woodworm (Furniture beetle larva)

I DON'T BELIEVE IT!

Animal droppings are delicious and tasty to many kinds of insects. Various types of beetles lay their eggs in warm and steamy piles of droppings. The larvae soon hatch out and eat the dung!

Capsid bug

Shield bug

Fruitfly

Lacebug

44 Insects even feed on old bits of damp and crumbling wood, dying trees, brown and decaying leaves and smelly, rotting fruit. They are not fussy eaters! This is nature's way of recycling goodness and nutrients in old plant parts, and returning them to the soil so new trees and other plants can grow.

Unwelcome guests

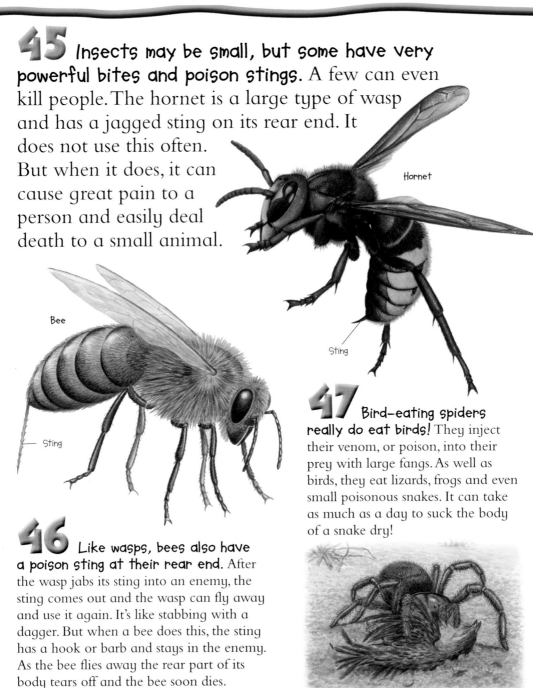

45 Insects may be small, but some have very powerful bites and poison stings. A few can even kill people. The hornet is a large type of wasp and has a jagged sting on its rear end. It does not use this often. But when it does, it can cause great pain to a person and easily deal death to a small animal.

Hornet

Sting

Bee

Sting

47 Bird-eating spiders really do eat birds! They inject their venom, or poison, into their prey with large fangs. As well as birds, they eat lizards, frogs and even small poisonous snakes. It can take as much as a day to suck the body of a snake dry!

46 Like wasps, bees also have a poison sting at their rear end. After the wasp jabs its sting into an enemy, the sting comes out and the wasp can fly away and use it again. It's like stabbing with a dagger. But when a bee does this, the sting has a hook or barb and stays in the enemy. As the bee flies away the rear part of its body tears off and the bee soon dies.

48 The bombardier beetle squirts out a spray of horrible liquid from its rear end, almost like a small spray–gun! This startles and stings the attacker and gives the small beetle time to escape.

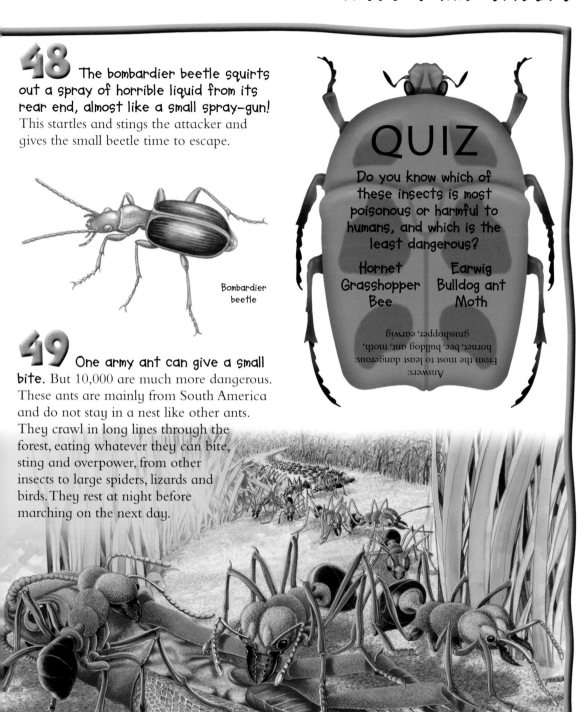

Bombardier beetle

QUIZ

Do you know which of these insects is most poisonous or harmful to humans, and which is the least dangerous?

Hornet   Earwig
Grasshopper   Bulldog ant
Bee   Moth

Answers:
From the most to least dangerous:
hornet, bee, bulldog ant, moth,
grasshopper, earwig

49 One army ant can give a small bite. But 10,000 are much more dangerous. These ants are mainly from South America and do not stay in a nest like other ants. They crawl in long lines through the forest, eating whatever they can bite, sting and overpower, from other insects to large spiders, lizards and birds. They rest at night before marching on the next day.

Towns for termites

50 Some insects live together in huge groups called colonies — which are like insect cities. There are four main types of insects which form colonies. One is the termites. The other three are all in the same insect subgroup and are bees, wasps and ants.

51 Some kinds of termites make their nests inside a huge pile of mud and earth called a termite mound. The termites build the mound from wet mud which goes hard in the hot sun. The main part of the nest is below ground level. It has hundreds of tunnels and chambers where the termites live, feed and breed.

▶ Termites mounds are incredibly complex constructions. They can reach 10 metres tall, and have air conditioning shafts built into them. These enable the termites to control the temperature of the nest to within one degree.

52 Inside the termite 'city' there are various groups of termites, with different kinds of work to do. Some tunnel into the soil and collect food such as tiny bits of plants. Others guard the entrance to the nest and bite any animals which try to enter. Some look after the eggs and young forms, or larvae.

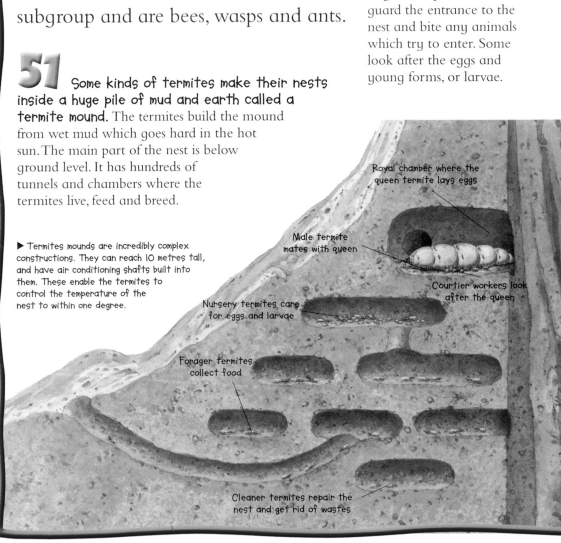

Royal chamber where the queen termite lays eggs

Male termite mates with queen

Courtier workers look after the queen

Nursery termites care for eggs and larvae

Forager termites collect food

Cleaner termites repair the nest and get rid of wastes

55 A wasp nest will have about 2000 wasps in it, but these are small builders in the insect world! A termite colony may have more than 5,000,000 inhabitants! Other insect colonies are smaller, although most have a similar set-up with one queen and various kinds of workers. Wood ants form nests of up to 300,000 and honeybees around 50,000. Some bumblebees live in colonies numbering only 10 or 20.

53 The queen termite is up to 100 times bigger than the workers. She is the only one in the nest who lays eggs – thousands every day.

54 Leafcutter ants grow their own food! They harvest leaves which they use at the nest to grow fungus, which they eat.

▼ When the sections of leaf are taken back to the nest, other ants cut them up into smaller sections. They are then used in gardens to grow the ants' food.

I DON'T BELIEVE IT!

Ants get milk from green cows! The 'cows' are really aphids. Ants look after the aphids. In return, when an ant strokes an aphid, the aphid oozes a drop of 'milk', a sugary liquid called honeydew, which the ant sips to get energy.

Where am I?

56 **Insects have some of the best types of camouflage in the whole world of animals.** Camouflage is when a living thing is coloured and patterned to blend in with its surroundings, so it is difficult to notice. This makes it hard for predators to see or find it. Or, if the insect is a predator itself, camouflage helps it to creep up unnoticed on prey.

58 **The thornbug has a hard, pointed body casing.** It sits still on a twig pretending to be a real thorn. It moves about and feeds at night.

57 **Stick and leaf insects look exactly like sticks and leaves.** The body and legs of a stick insect are long and twig-like. The body of a leaf insect has wide, flat parts which are coloured to resemble leaves. Both these types of insects eat plants. When the wind blows they rock and sway in the breeze, just like the real twigs and leaves around them.

Spiny stick insect

Rajah Brooke's bird-wing butterfly

Green Indian stick insect

59
Shieldbugs have broad, flat bodies that look like the leaves around them. The body is shaped like the shield carried by a medieval knight-in-armour.

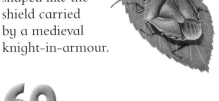

60
Many butterflies seem too brightly coloured to blend in with their surroundings. But when the wings are held together over the butterfly's back, the undersides show. These are usually brown or green – dark colours like the leaves.

Green Indian stick insect

Rajah Brooke's bird-wing butterfly

MAKE A CAMOUFLAGE SCENE

1. Carefully cut out a butterfly shape from stiff card. Colour it brightly with a bold pattern, such as yellow and brown spots on an orange background, or orange stripes on a blue background.

2. Cut out 10–20 leaf shapes from card. Colour them like your butterfly. Stick the leaves on a cardboard branch.

3. Your butterfly may seem far too bright and bold to be camouflaged. But put the butterfly on your branch. See how well its camouflage works now!

61
The bird-dropping caterpillar looks just like – a pile of bird's droppings! Not many animals would want to eat it, so it survives longer.

33

Great pretenders

62 Some insects pretend to be what they're not — especially other insects. For example, a hoverfly has a body with yellow and black stripes. At first sight it looks very similar to a wasp. But it is not. It is a type of fly and it is harmless. It cannot sting like a real wasp.

63 A mimic is an animal which, at a glance, looks similar to another animal, but which is really a different kind of creature. The animal which the mimic resembles is known as the model. Usually, the model is dangerous or harmful in some way. It may have a powerful bite or a poisonous sting. Other animals avoid it. Usually, the mimic is harmless. But it looks like the harmful model, so other animals avoid it too. The mimic gains safety or protection by looking like the model.

▲ The harmless hoverfly looks just like a wasp. Like other mimics, it fools other animals into thinking it is more dangerous than it is.

64 The hornet moth is a mimic of the large type of wasp known as the hornet. A hornet has a very painful sting and few other creatures dare to try and eat it. The hornet moth is harmless but few other creatures dare to eat it either.

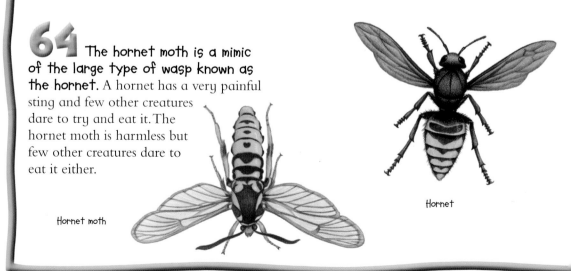

Hornet moth

Hornet

65 The monarch butterfly has bright, bold colours on its wings. These warn other animals, such as birds and lizards, that its flesh tastes horrible and is poisonous. The viceroy butterfly is very similar to the monarch but it is a mimic – its flesh is not distasteful. As well as being poisonous, the monarch is also a champion migrating insect.

Monarch butterfly

Viceroy butterfly

66 The bee fly cannot sting like a real bee. But it looks just like a bee, with a hairy striped body.

▶ The bee fly avoids predators by looking like a bee.

67 The ant-beetle resembles an ant, although it does not have a strong bite and a sting like a real ant. The ant-beetle enters the ant's nest and steals ant larvae to eat.

QUIZ
Sort these models and mimics into pairs where the harmless mimic looks like the harmful model.

Mimic	Model
Ant-beetle	Hornet
Bee fly	Ant
Hornet moth	Bee
Hoverfly	Monarch
Viceroy	Wasp

Answer:
Ant-beetle and ant; bee fly and bee;
Hornet moth and hornet; hoverfly and
wasp; viceroy and monarch.

35

Stay or go?

68 The cold of winter or the dryness of drought are hard times for most animals, including insects. How can they survive? One answer is to hibernate. Many insects find a safe, sheltered place and go to sleep. Butterflies crawl behind creepers and vines. Ladybirds cluster in thick bushes. Beetles dig into the soil or among tree roots. However, these insects are not really asleep in the way that you go to sleep. They are simply too cold to move. As the weather becomes warmer, they become active again.

69 Some insects migrate, travel long distances to somewhere conditions are better. Some insects do this only when they become too numerous. After a few years of good conditions in Africa, locusts (a type of large grasshopper) increase in numbers so much they form vast swarms of millions. With so many locusts together, they eat all the food in a whole area and fly off to look for more. They eat massive areas of farm crops and people are left to starve.

Peacock butterfly

Ladybird

Squash beetle

▲ All these insects hibernate through winter each year.

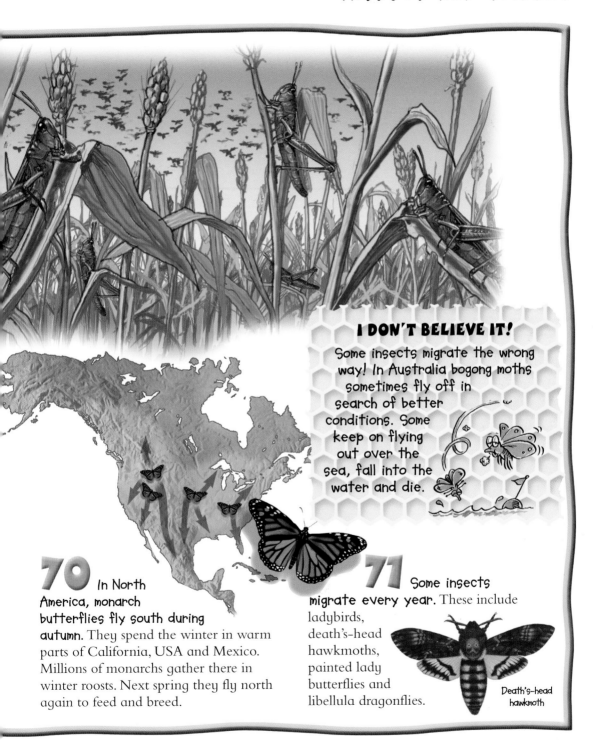

70 In North America, monarch butterflies fly south during autumn. They spend the winter in warm parts of California, USA and Mexico. Millions of monarchs gather there in winter roosts. Next spring they fly north again to feed and breed.

71 Some insects migrate every year. These include ladybirds, death's-head hawkmoths, painted lady butterflies and libellula dragonflies.

Death's-head hawkmoth

Noisy neighbours

72 The tropical forest is warm and still – but far from quiet. Many insects are making chirps, buzzes, clicks, screeches, hums and other noises. Most are males, making their songs or calls to attract females at breeding time.

73 Some of the noisiest insects are cicadas, plant-eating bugs with large wings. The male cicada has two thin patches of body casing, one on either side of its abdomen (rear body part). Tiny muscles pull in each patch, then let it go again, like clicking a tin lid in and out. This happens very fast and the clicks merge into a buzzing sound which can be heard one kilometre away.

Giant wood wasp

Great green bush cricket

Mole cricket

Cicada

Garden tiger moth

Deathwatch beetle

Cockchafer

Click beetle

Screech beetle

QUIZ

1. What is a locust?
2. Which butterflies spend the summer in California, USA and Mexico?
3. Do monarch butterflies hibernate through winter?
4. What do cicadas eat?
5. How did mole crickets get their name?

Answers:
1. A type of large grasshopper.
2. Monarch butterflies. 3. No, they migrate. 4. Plants. 5. They burrow like moles.

74 Like most other crickets, the male katydid chirps by rubbing together his wings. The bases of the wings near the body have hard, ridged strips like rows of pegs. These click past each other to make the chirping sound.

75 The male mole cricket chirps in a similar way. But he also sits at the entrance to his burrow in the soil. (Mole crickets get their name from the way they tunnel through soil, like real moles.) The burrow entrance is specially shaped, almost like the loudspeaker of a music system. It makes the chirps sound louder and travel farther.

Meet the family!

76 Are all minibeasts, bugs and creepy-crawlies truly insects? One way to tell is to count the legs. If a creature has six legs, it's an insect. If it has fewer or more, it's some other kind of animal. However, leg-counting only works with fully-grown or adult creatures. Some young forms or larvae, like fly maggots, have no legs at all. But they develop into six-legged flies, and flies are certainly insects.

Maggots

Tick

Mite

77 Mites and ticks have eight legs. They are not insects. Ticks and some mites cling onto larger animals and suck their blood. Some mites are so small that a handful of soil may contain half a million of them. Mites and ticks belong to the group of animals with eight legs, called arachnids. Other arachnids are spiders and scorpions.

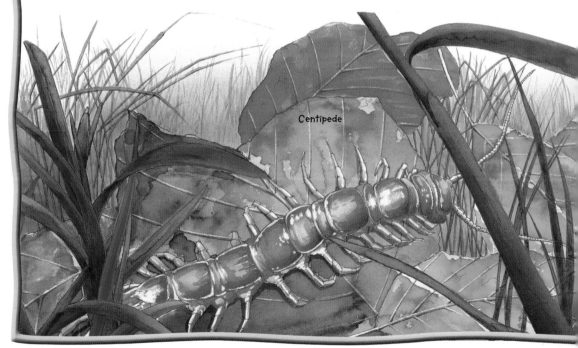

Centipede

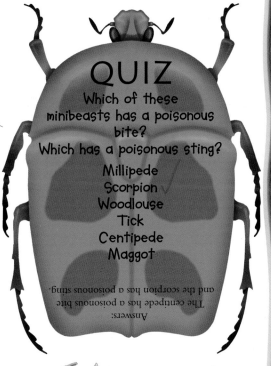

78 A woodlouse has a hard body casing and feelers on its head. But it has more than ten legs so it is certainly not an insect! It is a crustacean – a cousin of crabs and lobsters.

79 Centipedes have lots of legs, far more than six – usually over 30. The centipede has two very long fangs that give a poison bite. It races across the ground hunting for small animals to eat – such as insects.

80 Millipedes have 50 or 100 legs, maybe even more. They are certainly not insects. Millipedes eat bits of plants such as old leaves, bark and wood.

QUIZ

Which of these minibeasts has a poisonous bite? Which has a poisonous sting?

Millipede
Scorpion
Woodlouse
Tick
Centipede
Maggot

Answers:
The centipede has a poisonous bite and the scorpion has a poisonous sting.

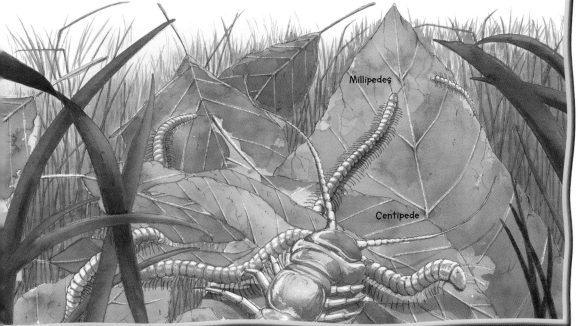

Millipedes

Centipede

Silky spiders

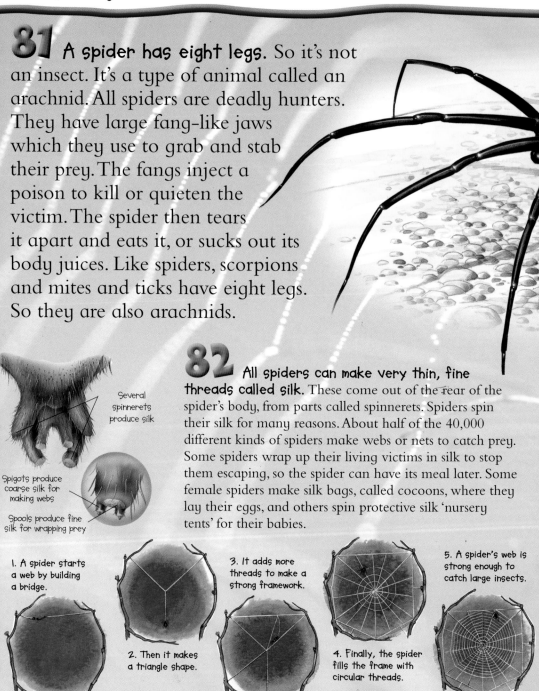

81 **A spider has eight legs.** So it's not an insect. It's a type of animal called an arachnid. All spiders are deadly hunters. They have large fang-like jaws which they use to grab and stab their prey. The fangs inject a poison to kill or quieten the victim. The spider then tears it apart and eats it, or sucks out its body juices. Like spiders, scorpions and mites and ticks have eight legs. So they are also arachnids.

Several spinnerets produce silk

Spigots produce coarse silk for making webs

Spools produce fine silk for wrapping prey

82 **All spiders can make very thin, fine threads called silk.** These come out of the rear of the spider's body, from parts called spinnerets. Spiders spin their silk for many reasons. About half of the 40,000 different kinds of spiders make webs or nets to catch prey. Some spiders wrap up their living victims in silk to stop them escaping, so the spider can have its meal later. Some female spiders make silk bags, called cocoons, where they lay their eggs, and others spin protective silk 'nursery tents' for their babies.

1. A spider starts a web by building a bridge.

2. Then it makes a triangle shape.

3. It adds more threads to make a strong framework.

4. Finally, the spider fills the frame with circular threads.

5. A spider's web is strong enough to catch large insects.

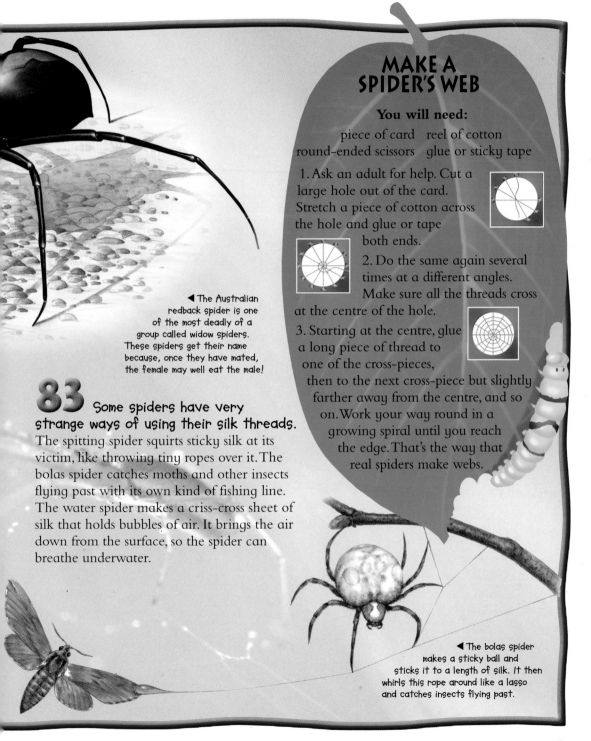

◀ The Australian redback spider is one of the most deadly of a group called widow spiders. These spiders get their name because, once they have mated, the female may well eat the male!

83
Some spiders have very strange ways of using their silk threads. The spitting spider squirts sticky silk at its victim, like throwing tiny ropes over it. The bolas spider catches moths and other insects flying past with its own kind of fishing line. The water spider makes a criss-cross sheet of silk that holds bubbles of air. It brings the air down from the surface, so the spider can breathe underwater.

MAKE A SPIDER'S WEB

You will need:

piece of card   reel of cotton
round-ended scissors   glue or sticky tape

1. Ask an adult for help. Cut a large hole out of the card. Stretch a piece of cotton across the hole and glue or tape both ends.

2. Do the same again several times at a different angles. Make sure all the threads cross at the centre of the hole.

3. Starting at the centre, glue a long piece of thread to one of the cross-pieces, then to the next cross-piece but slightly farther away from the centre, and so on. Work your way round in a growing spiral until you reach the edge. That's the way that real spiders make webs.

◀ The bolas spider makes a sticky ball and sticks it to a length of silk. It then whirls this rope around like a lasso and catches insects flying past.

Inventive arachnids

84 Not all spiders catch their prey using webs. Wolf spiders are strong and have long legs. They run fast and chase tiny prey such as beetles, caterpillars and slugs.

Wolf spider

86 The trapdoor spider lives in a burrow with a wedge-shaped door made from silk. The spider hides just behind this door. When it detects a small animal passing, it opens the door and rushes out to grab its victim.

▶ This gold leaf crab spider has caught a honeybee. Its venom works fast to paralyse the bee. If it did not, the bee's struggling might harm the spider and draw the attention of the spider's enemies.

85 The crab spider looks like a small crab, with a wide, tubby body and curved legs. It usually sits on a flower which is the same colour as itself. It keeps very still so it is camouflaged – it merges in with its surroundings. Small insects such as flies, beetles and bees come to the flower to gather food and the crab spider pounces on them.

▼ The eyes of the tiny jumping spider work like a zoom lens on a camera, and help it judge distances very well.

87 The jumping spider is only 5–10 millimetres long – but it can leap more than 20 times this distance. It jumps onto tiny prey such as ants. The jumping spider's eyes are enormous for its small body, so it can see how far it needs to leap so that it lands on its victim.

88 Bird–eating spiders, sometimes called 'tarantulas', are huge, hairy spiders from tropical South America and Africa. Stretch out your hand and it still would not be as big as some of these giants. They are strong enough to catch big beetles, grasshoppers, other spiders and even mice, frogs, lizards and small birds.

I DON'T BELIEVE IT!

The name 'tarantula' was first given to a type of wolf spider from Europe. Its body is about 40 millimetres long and it lives in a burrow. Its bite can be very irritating, sore and painful.

▶ This tarantula has caught a katydid, a type of grasshopper.

A sting in the tail

89 A scorpion has eight legs. It is not an insect. Like a spider, it is an arachnid. Scorpions live in warm parts of the world. Some are at home in dripping rainforests. Others like baking deserts. The scorpion has large, crab-like pincers, called pedipalps, to grab its prey, and powerful jaws like scissors to chop it up.

90 The scorpion has a dangerous poison sting at the tip of its tail. It may use this to poison or paralyse a victim, so the victim cannot move. Or the scorpion may wave its tail at enemies to warn them that, unless they go away, it will sting them to death!

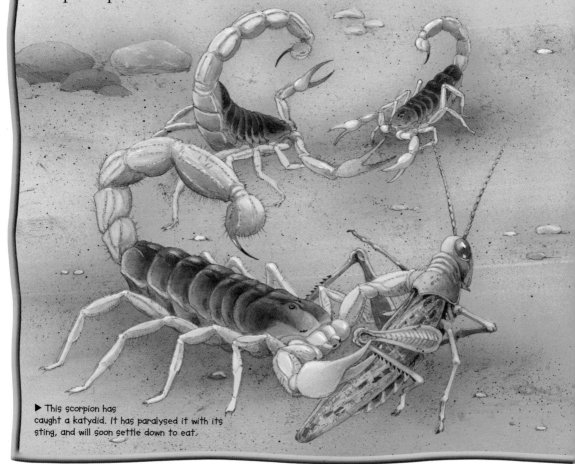

▶ This scorpion has caught a katydid. It has paralysed it with its sting, and will soon settle down to eat.

91 The sun spider or solifuge is another very fierce, eight-legged, spider-like hunter, with a poisonous bite. It lives in deserts and dry places, which is why it's sometimes called the camel spider.

92 The false scorpion looks like a scorpion, with big pincers. But it does not have a poisonous sting in its tail. It doesn't even have a tail. And it's tiny – it could fit into this 'O'! It lives in the soil and hunts even smaller creatures.

King crab

93 A crab may seem an odd cousin for a spider or scorpion. But the horseshoe or king crab is very unusual. It has eight legs – so it's an arachnid. It also has a large domed shell and strong spiky tail. There were horseshoe crabs in the seas well before dinosaurs roamed the land.

QUIZ

Look though this book and decide which of these animals are NOT insects. How can you tell – by counting the legs? Not always!

Beetle   Millipede
Caterpillar   Scorpion
Cricket   Scorpionfly
King crab   Slug
Louse   Tarantula

Answers
They are all insects apart from the king crab, millipede, scorpion, slug and the tarantula

94 Animals don't have to be big to be dangerous. These spiders are both very poisonous and their bites can even kill people. This is why you should never mess about with spiders or poke your hands into holes and dark places!

Violin spider

Black widow spider

Friends and foes

95 Some insects are harmful – but others are very helpful. They are a vital part of the natural world. Flies, butterflies, beetles and many others visit flowers to collect nectar and pollen to eat. In the process they carry pollen from flower to flower. This is called pollination and is needed so that the flower can form seeds or fruits.

96 Spiders are very helpful to gardeners. They catch lots of insect pests, like flies, in their webs.

97 Bees make honey, sweet and sticky and packed with energy. People keep honeybees in hives so the honey is easier to collect. Wild bees make honey to feed their larvae and as a food store when conditions are bad. But the honey is eaten by numerous animals such as bears, ratels (honey-badgers) and birds.

◀ These bees are busy working in their hive. On the right you can see the young, c-shaped grubs.

98 **A few kinds of insects are among the most harmful creatures in the world.** They do not attack and kill people directly, like tigers and crocodiles. But they do spread many types of dangerous diseases such as malaria.

99 **When blood-sucking flies such as mosquitoes bite someone with malaria, they suck in a small amount of blood.** This contains millions of microscopic germs which cause the disease. As the fly bites another person, a tiny drop of the first person's blood gets into the second person – and the disease is passed on.

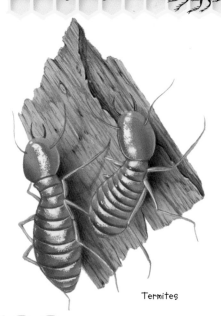

Termites

100 **Some insects even damage wooden houses, bridges, barns and walkways.** Certain kinds of termites make nests in the wood and tunnel inside it. The damage cannot be seen from the outside until the timber is eaten almost hollow. Then it collapses into a pile of dust if anyone even touches it!

Sharks swarm the seas

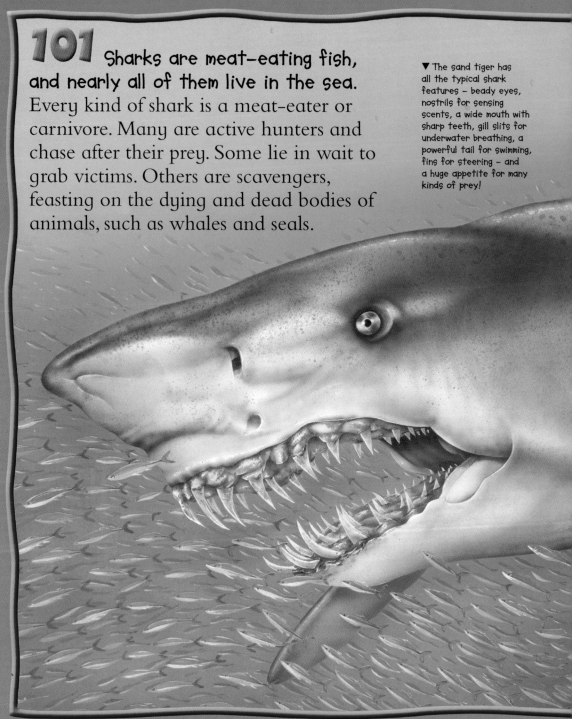

101 Sharks are meat—eating fish, and nearly all of them live in the sea. Every kind of shark is a meat-eater or carnivore. Many are active hunters and chase after their prey. Some lie in wait to grab victims. Others are scavengers, feasting on the dying and dead bodies of animals, such as whales and seals.

▼ The sand tiger has all the typical shark features – beady eyes, nostrils for sensing scents, a wide mouth with sharp teeth, gill slits for underwater breathing, a powerful tail for swimming, fins for steering – and a huge appetite for many kinds of prey!

Some sharks are giants

102 **The biggest fish in the world is a type of shark called the whale shark.** It grows to 12 metres long, about the same as three family cars end-to-end. It can weigh over 12 tonnes, which is three times heavier than three family cars put together!

103 **Despite the whale shark's huge size, it mostly eats tiny prey.** It opens its enormous mouth, takes in a great gulp of water and squeezes it out through the gill slits on either side of its neck. Inside the gills, small animals such as shrimp-like krill, little fish and baby squid are trapped and swallowed.

▶ Krill look like small shrimps and are usually 2 to 3 centimetres long. Millions of them, along with other small creatures, make up plankton.

104 **Whale sharks like cruising across the warm oceans, swimming up to 5000 kilometres in one year.** They wander far and wide, but tend to visit the same areas at certain times of year, when their food is plentiful.

▲ The whale shark swims with its mouth wide open to filter krill from the water. It sometimes swallows larger animals, such as penguins, smaller sharks and tuna fish.

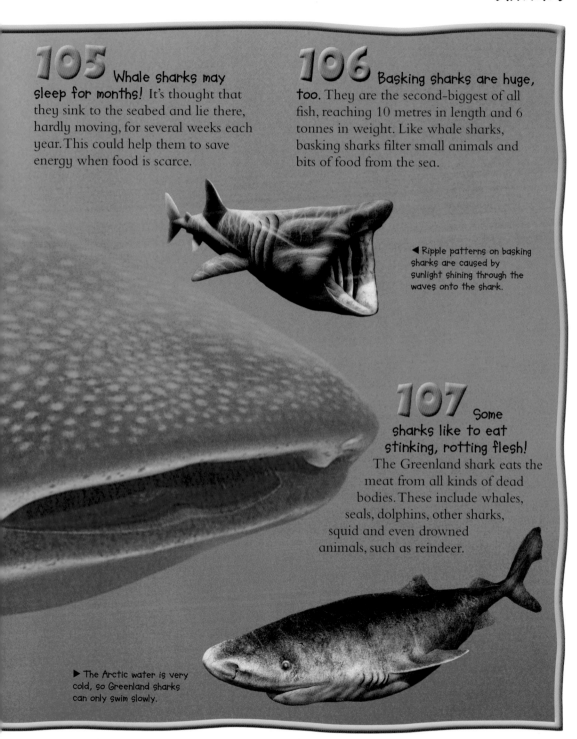

105 Whale sharks may sleep for months! It's thought that they sink to the seabed and lie there, hardly moving, for several weeks each year. This could help them to save energy when food is scarce.

106 Basking sharks are huge, too. They are the second-biggest of all fish, reaching 10 metres in length and 6 tonnes in weight. Like whale sharks, basking sharks filter small animals and bits of food from the sea.

◄ Ripple patterns on basking sharks are caused by sunlight shining through the waves onto the shark.

107 Some sharks like to eat stinking, rotting flesh! The Greenland shark eats the meat from all kinds of dead bodies. These include whales, seals, dolphins, other sharks, squid and even drowned animals, such as reindeer.

► The Arctic water is very cold, so Greenland sharks can only swim slowly.

Sharks outlived the dinosaurs.

108 **The first sharks lived more than 350 million years ago.** This was 120 million years before the dinosaurs appeared on Earth. Dinosaurs died out 65 million years ago but sharks survived. So sharks have ruled the seas for over twice as long as dinosaurs ruled the land!

109 **Some prehistoric fish are called 'spiny sharks'.** They looked like sharks with streamlined bodies and sharp spikes on their fins and bellies. Their real name is acanthodians, and they lived in lakes and rivers 400 to 250 million years ago.

MAKE MEGALODON'S MOUTH!

You will need:
black pen   big cardboard box
large pieces of white card
scissors   tape
1. Use a pen to draw a shark's mouth
onto the box and cut it out.
2. Draw and cut out 20 teeth shapes.
3. Tape these inside the mouth.
Draw on eyes. Now you can
stare *Megalodon*
in the face!

◀ Sharks' basic body shapes and behaviour have hardly changed since they first appeared. The shark *Hybodus* lived about 160 million years ago in the Jurassic period, during the age of dinosaurs.

110 **Bits of shark have turned to stone!** Parts of sharks that died long ago have been preserved in rocks, as fossils. Most fossils are made of the hard parts, such as teeth and scales. These show the size of the shark and the kind of food it ate.

◀ *Megalodon* was probably similar in shape to the great white shark of today.

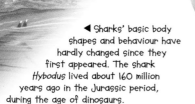

111 **The biggest shark in history was probably *Megalodon*.** Its fossil teeth look like those of the great white shark, but they're twice as big. *Megalodon* could have been 15 or even 20 metres long – three times the size of today's great white. It lived about 20 to 2 million years ago and was one of the greatest hunters the animal world has ever known.

Super swimmers

112 Nearly all sharks are slim and streamlined, making them fast swimmers. A streamlined shape slips through the water easily and lets the shark travel at speed. One of the fastest sharks is the shortfin mako. It swims at more than 55 kilometres an hour – much faster than a champion human sprinter!

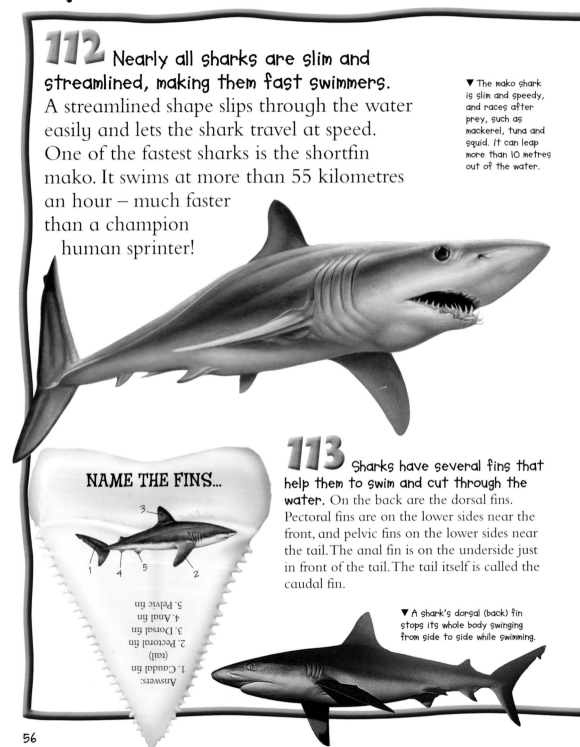

▼ The mako shark is slim and speedy, and races after prey, such as mackerel, tuna and squid. It can leap more than 10 metres out of the water.

NAME THE FINS...

3
1   4   5   2

Answers:
1. Caudal fin (tail)
2. Pectoral fin
3. Dorsal fin
4. Anal fin
5. Pelvic fin

113 Sharks have several fins that help them to swim and cut through the water. On the back are the dorsal fins. Pectoral fins are on the lower sides near the front, and pelvic fins on the lower sides near the tail. The anal fin is on the underside just in front of the tail. The tail itself is called the caudal fin.

▼ A shark's dorsal (back) fin stops its whole body swinging from side to side while swimming.

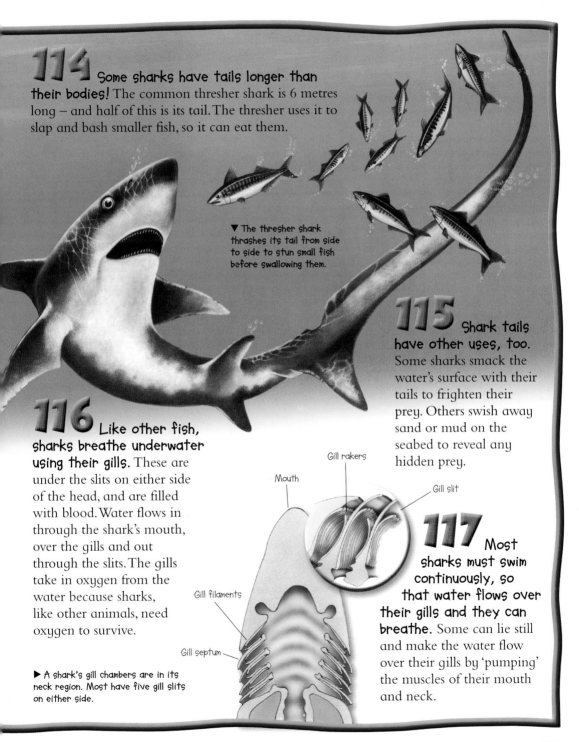

114 Some sharks have tails longer than their bodies! The common thresher shark is 6 metres long – and half of this is its tail. The thresher uses it to slap and bash smaller fish, so it can eat them.

▼ The thresher shark thrashes its tail from side to side to stun small fish before swallowing them.

115 Shark tails have other uses, too. Some sharks smack the water's surface with their tails to frighten their prey. Others swish away sand or mud on the seabed to reveal any hidden prey.

116 Like other fish, sharks breathe underwater using their gills. These are under the slits on either side of the head, and are filled with blood. Water flows in through the shark's mouth, over the gills and out through the slits. The gills take in oxygen from the water because sharks, like other animals, need oxygen to survive.

Gill rakers

Mouth

Gill slit

Gill filaments

Gill septum

117 Most sharks must swim continuously, so that water flows over their gills and they can breathe. Some can lie still and make the water flow over their gills by 'pumping' the muscles of their mouth and neck.

▶ A shark's gill chambers are in its neck region. Most have five gill slits on either side.

Sharks eat almost anything!

118 **Tiger sharks swallow all kinds of rubbish.** This shark is famous for trying to eat nearly everything, in the hope that it might be tasty. However, some of the items it swallows are not even food — such as tin cans and beach shoes!

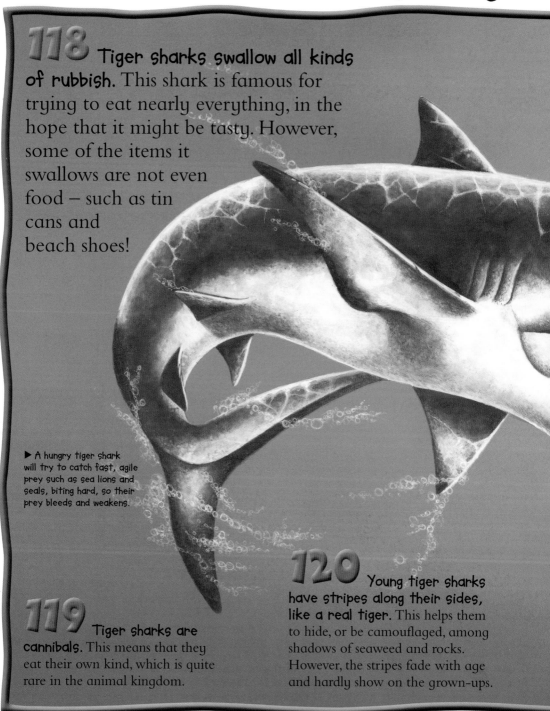

▶ A hungry tiger shark will try to catch fast, agile prey such as sea lions and seals, biting hard, so their prey bleeds and weakens.

119 **Tiger sharks are cannibals.** This means that they eat their own kind, which is quite rare in the animal kingdom.

120 **Young tiger sharks have stripes along their sides, like a real tiger.** This helps them to hide, or be camouflaged, among shadows of seaweed and rocks. However, the stripes fade with age and hardly show on the grown-ups.

121 Tiger sharks swim right up to the beach! Most sharks stay away from the shore in case they get stranded and die. But tiger sharks come near to the shore, especially at night, to explore for food. They don't seem to mind swimming in water that's so shallow, it would hardly cover your knees. This can make it dangerous to go paddling!

I DON'T BELIEVE IT!
Tiger sharks have eaten all kinds of strange things — bottles, tools, car tyres, and in one case, a type of drum called a tom-tom!

122 Most sharks prefer just a few types of food. One kind of bullhead shark likes to eat only sea urchins. However, if it gets very hungry, it will try other foods.

123 Not all sharks have sharp, pointed teeth. The Port Jackson shark has wide, broad teeth, like rounded pebbles. It uses these to crush the hard body cases of its favourite food — shellfish.

Sharks have no bones!

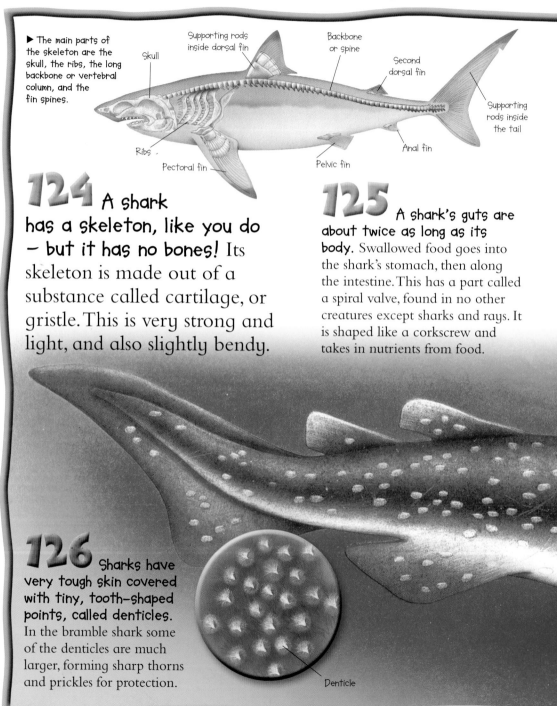

▶ The main parts of the skeleton are the skull, the ribs, the long backbone or vertebral column, and the fin spines.

Skull

Supporting rods inside dorsal fin

Backbone or spine

Second dorsal fin

Supporting rods inside the tail

Ribs

Pectoral fin

Pelvic fin

Anal fin

124 **A shark has a skeleton, like you do – but it has no bones!** Its skeleton is made out of a substance called cartilage, or gristle. This is very strong and light, and also slightly bendy.

125 **A shark's guts are about twice as long as its body.** Swallowed food goes into the shark's stomach, then along the intestine. This has a part called a spiral valve, found in no other creatures except sharks and rays. It is shaped like a corkscrew and takes in nutrients from food.

126 **Sharks have very tough skin covered with tiny, tooth-shaped points, called denticles.** In the bramble shark some of the denticles are much larger, forming sharp thorns and prickles for protection.

Denticle

127 Shark skin can be useful.
Through the ages it has been used by people as a strong material to make handbags, shoes, belts, cases, handle grips and even a special kind of sandpaper known as chagrin.

▲ Shark products such as bags and even vitamin pills have been made for centuries, but today many sharks are rare and need protecting.

WHICH BODY BITS ARE...
A. Inside a shark but not inside you?
B. Inside you but not inside a shark?
C. Inside you and a shark?
1. Stomach
2. Lungs
3. Spiral valve
4. Liver
5. Gills

Answers:
1.C 2.B
3.A 4.C
5.A

128 Many sharks produce slime.
The slime made by the skin slides off easily and helps the shark to swim faster. New slime is always being made quickly by the skin to replace the slime that flows away. If a shark is trapped in a net, it thrashes about and tries to escape. This can damage the slime layer and cause cuts and sores on the skin.

▲ The bramble shark is very 'thorny', studded with extra-large denticles. It is a slow swimmer and grows to 4 metres long.

Ultimate killer

129 The world's biggest predatory, or hunting, fish is the great white shark. In real life it is certainly large — at 6 metres in length and weighing more than one tonne. Great whites live around the world, mainly in warmer seas. They have a fearsome reputation.

▼ Great whites are curious about unfamiliar items in the sea. They often come very close to investigate anti-shark cages and the divers protected inside. This is partly because great whites are always on the lookout for food.

I DON'T BELIEVE IT!

The risk of being struck by lightning is 20 times greater than the risk of being attacked by a shark.

130 Great whites get hot! This is because they can make their bodies warmer than the surrounding water. This allows their muscles to work more quickly, so they can swim faster and more powerfully. It means the great white is partly 'warm-blooded' like you.

131 The great white has 50 or more teeth and each one is up to 6 centimetres long. The teeth are razor-sharp but slim, like blades, and they sometimes snap off. But new teeth are always growing just behind, ready to move forward and replace the snapped-off teeth.

132 The great white often attacks unseen from below. It surges up from the dark depths with tremendous power. It can smash into a big prey such as a seal or a dolphin, and lift it right out of the water as it takes its first bite.

133 Great whites let their victims bleed to death. They bite on their first charge then move off, leaving the victim with terrible wounds. When the injured prey is weak, the great white comes back to devour its meal.

134 The great white 'saws' lumps of food from its victim. Each tooth has tiny sharp points along its edges. As the shark starts to feed, it bites hard and then shakes its head from side to side. The teeth work like rows of small saws to slice off a mouthful.

Strange sharks

135 **Six-gill sharks have an extra pair of gills.** This may be the number that ancient sharks had long ago, before they developed into modern sharks. Six-gill sharks are up to 5 metres long and eat various foods, from shellfish to dead dolphins.

▶ Each tooth of the frilled shark has three needle-like points for grabbing soft-bodied prey.

I DON'T BELIEVE IT!

The smallest sharks could lie curled up in your hand. The dwarf lanternshark is just 20 centimetres long.

136 **Some sharks are frilly.** The frilled shark has six pairs of wavy gill slits. It looks more like an eel than a shark, with a slim body 2 metres in length, and long frilly fins. It is dark brown in colour, lives in very deep waters and eats squid and octopus.

137
Some sharks look like unicorns – especially the goblin shark. It has a very long, pointed snout that looks like the horn on the head of the mythical horse-like beast called the unicorn. Goblin sharks grow up to 3 metres in length.

138
The saw shark has a 'saw' for a nose. Its long nose, or snout, is up to half its total length. The snout has teeth-like points sticking out from the sides. The shark uses its snout to dig around in sand and mud for prey, such as shellfish.

◄ A saw shark may lose and re-grow as many as 30,000 teeth during its lifetime.

139
Some sharks glow in the dark – especially lanternsharks. They live in deep dark water and have glowing spots on their bodies, particularly around their mouths and along their sides. The spots may attract curious small creatures such as fish and squid, so the shark can snap them up.

► The lanternshark's tiny light-producing organs are called photophores.

Sharks are sensitive!

140 Most sharks have big eyes and can see well, especially in the dark. Many feed at night, or in deeper water where there's little light. This makes eyesight especially important to the shark so that it can spot its prey. Some sharks have eyes that glow in the dark, like a cat's.

▼ A porbeagle shark uses its keen eyesight to chase its favourite food — mackerel.

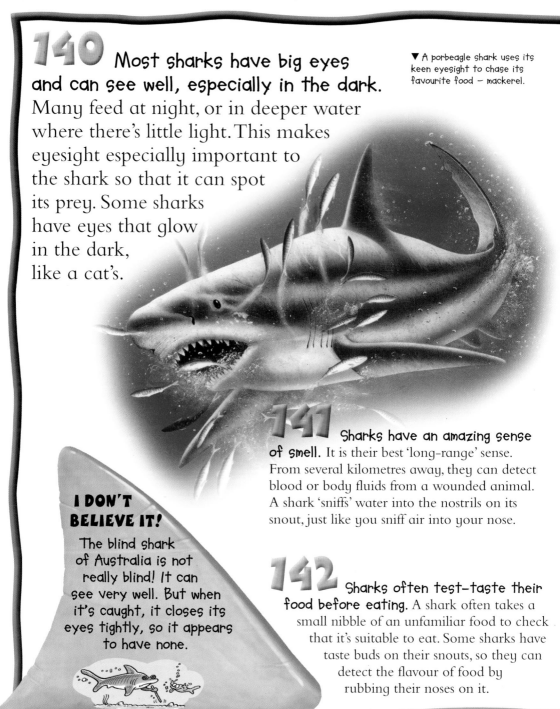

141 Sharks have an amazing sense of smell. It is their best 'long-range' sense. From several kilometres away, they can detect blood or body fluids from a wounded animal. A shark 'sniffs' water into the nostrils on its snout, just like you sniff air into your nose.

I DON'T BELIEVE IT!

The blind shark of Australia is not really blind! It can see very well. But when it's caught, it closes its eyes tightly, so it appears to have none.

142 Sharks often test-taste their food before eating. A shark often takes a small nibble of an unfamiliar food to check that it's suitable to eat. Some sharks have taste buds on their snouts, so they can detect the flavour of food by rubbing their noses on it.

143 **Sharks can feel their way through narrow gaps in the dark using the sense of touch on their skin.** There is also a narrow strip along each side of a shark's body called the lateral line. It can sense ripples and currents in the water from animals moving nearby.

Lateral line

▲ The lateral line runs along the side of the body from head to tail base.

144 **Sharks can hear divers breathing!** They detect the sound of air bubbles coming from scuba-divers' mouths. But hearing is not the shark's best sense. Its ear openings are tiny, usually just behind the eyes.

▼ The electricity-sensing ampullae of Lorenzini show up as tiny holes over this great white's snout.

145 **Sharks can detect electricity.** As sea animals move, their muscles give off tiny pulses of electricity into the water. A shark has hundreds of tiny pits over its snout called ampullae of Lorenzini. These 'feel' the electric pulses. A shark can even detect prey buried out of sight in mud.

Hammers for heads

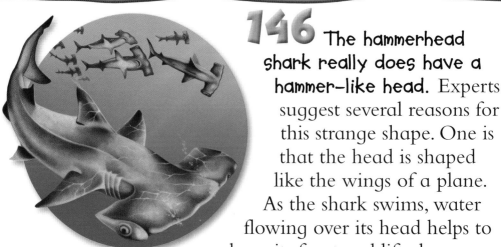

▲ The hammerhead's eyes, nostrils and electricity-sensing organs are at each end of the wing-shaped head.

146 **The hammerhead shark really does have a hammer-like head.** Experts suggest several reasons for this strange shape. One is that the head is shaped like the wings of a plane. As the shark swims, water flowing over its head helps to keep its front end lifted up, rather than nose-diving – just as wings keep a plane in the air.

147 **The hammer-shaped head may improve the shark's senses.** The nostrils are at each end of the 'hammer'. Smells drifting from the side reach one nostril well before the other. By swinging its head from side to side, the hammerhead can pinpoint the direction of a smell more quickly.

▼ Hammerheads often swim close to the seabed, searching for buried fish and shellfish.

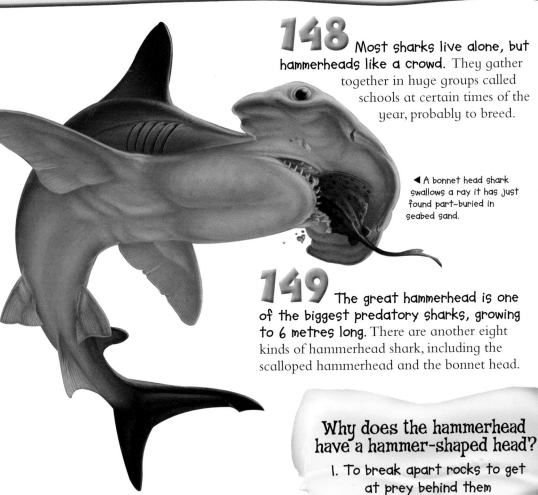

148 Most sharks live alone, but hammerheads like a crowd. They gather together in huge groups called schools at certain times of the year, probably to breed.

◀ A bonnet head shark swallows a ray it has just found part-buried in seabed sand.

149 The great hammerhead is one of the biggest predatory sharks, growing to 6 metres long. There are another eight kinds of hammerhead shark, including the scalloped hammerhead and the bonnet head.

Why does the hammerhead have a hammer-shaped head?

1. To break apart rocks to get at prey behind them
2. To help sense the direction of smells in the water
3. To smash open windows in shipwrecks.

Answer: 2

150 Hammerheads are among the most dangerous sharks. They have been known to attack people, although their usual food includes fish, squid, crabs and shellfish. They eat stingrays too and don't seem to be affected by the painful sting. However, hammerheads are themselves eaten – by people. They are caught and cut up for their tasty meat and for the thick oil from their livers.

Big mouth

151 The megamouth shark was discovered in 1976 near Hawaii in the Pacific Ocean. An American research ship hauled in its parachute-like anchor to find a strange shark tangled in it. Experts knew at once that this was a new type of shark, never described before.

153 Megamouths open their great mouths as they swim through shoals of small sea creatures, such as krill and young fish. The little prey get trapped inside the mouth and swallowed. The megamouth is not really an active hunter. It is a slow-swimming filter-feeder, like the whale shark and the basking shark.

152 The megamouth, as its name suggests, has a massive mouth more than 1.3 metres wide. Its soft, flabby body is about 5 metres long. In the summer when the megamouth has been feeding well, it can weigh more than one tonne.

154 **Megamouths go up and down every day.** They rise near the surface at dusk in order to feed during the night. At dawn they sink to deeper waters and spend the day in the dark, more than 200 metres down.

155 **Megamouths are scattered around the world.** They have been caught in all the tropical oceans, especially in the Western Pacific and Indian oceans. Only 20 or so have been found in the past 30 years. It may be that there have never been many megamouths in the world.

▼ The megamouth's huge jaws are right at the front of its body, not slung under the head as in most sharks.

The megamouth's mouth glows in the dark depths of the sea. Despite the vast size of the mouth the teeth are tiny

156 **Scientists believe that there may be more types of shark as yet undiscovered.** Sometimes the badly-rotted bodies of strange sharks are washed up onto beaches. But the remains are often too decayed to be identified.

The loose skin and floppy fins show that the megamouth is a slow swimmer

Swimming with sharks

▼ This great white shark is about to take a bite out of a piece of meat dangled from a boat. Although it's not hunting, you can see how it lifts its snout up high and thrusts its teeth forward to attack.

157 Some small types of shark are fairly safe and people can swim near them with care. In some tourist areas, people can even feed sharks. The sharks seem to become trained to accept food from divers.

158 The cookie-cutter shark is only 50 centimetres long, with a large mouth and big, sharp teeth. This shark attacks fish much larger than itself, biting out small patches of skin and flesh, before racing away. Its victim is left with a neat round hole on its body – ouch!

159 Some sharks get so used to accepting food from people that they get out of the habit of hunting. When the people are no longer around, the shark starts to starve.

160 Feeding and touching sharks is now banned in some places. Sometimes a shark snatches and swallows the food while it's still in a bag or net. This could give the shark bad stomach-ache, or even kill it. Also, touching sharks and other fish can damage their delicate skin, scales and layers of body slime. Finally, using meat to feed small, harmless sharks could attract bigger, dangerous ones.

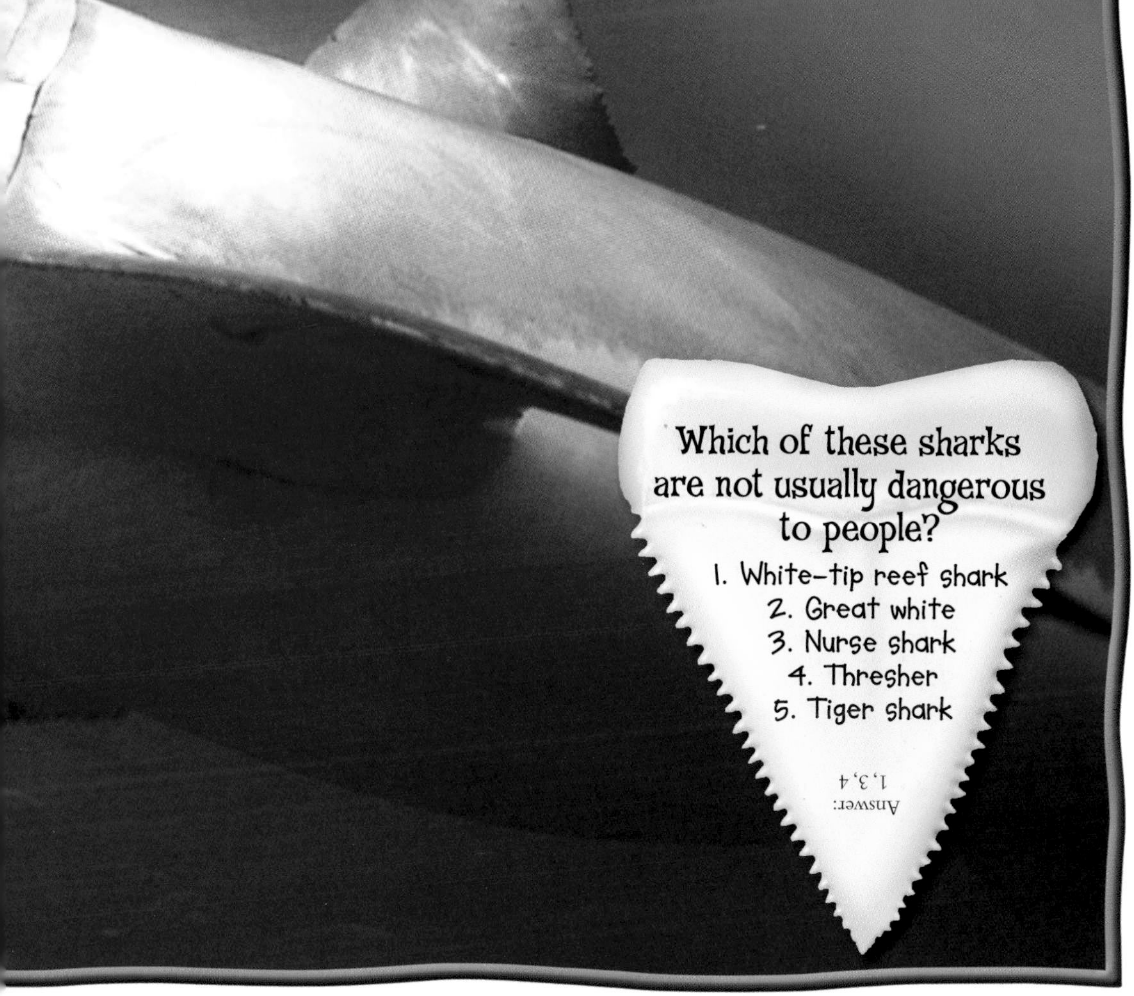

Which of these sharks are not usually dangerous to people?

1. White-tip reef shark
2. Great white
3. Nurse shark
4. Thresher
5. Tiger shark

Answer:
1, 3, 4

Shark cousins

161 **Sharks have many close relations who, like themselves, have a skeleton made of cartilage rather than bone.** Other kinds of cartilaginous fish include skates and rays, and the deep-water ratfish, or chimaera.

162 **Skates and rays are flat fish, but not flatfish.** True flatfish, such as plaice, have bony skeletons and lie on their left or right side. Skates and rays have very wide bodies with flattened upper and lower surfaces, and a long narrow tail.

▲ Chimaeras are also called ratfish after their long, tapering tails. Most are about one metre long.

163 **A ray or skate 'flies' through the water.** The sides of its body extend out like wings. The 'wings' push the water backwards, and so the ray or skate swims forwards. Unlike sharks and other fish, the ray's tail is seldom used for swimming.

▶ The huge manta ray has fleshy side flaps or 'horns' on its head that guide water into its mouth. It is shown here with a smaller and more common type of ray, the spotted eagle ray.

Spotted eagle ray

164 **The biggest rays are mantas.** They measure up to 7 metres across and weigh nearly 2 tonnes. Manta rays have huge mouths and feed like whale sharks by filtering small creatures from the water. Despite their great size, mantas can leap clear of the surface and crash back with a tremendous splash.

165 **Stingrays have sharp spines on their long tails.** They use them like daggers to jab poison into enemies or victims. Some stingrays live in lakes and rivers.

166 **Sawfish are different from saw-sharks.** A sawfish is shaped like a shark, but is a type of ray with a long snout edged by pointed teeth. You can tell the difference between them because a sawfish has gill slits on the bottom of its body, rather than on the side.

Manta ray

THE 'FLYING' RAY

You will need:
scissors stiff paper coloured pens
sticky tape drinking straw
modelling clay

1. Cut out a ray shape from paper.
2. Colour it brightly. Fold it along the middle so the 'wings' angle upwards. Stick the straw along the underside, so part sticks out as a 'tail'. Add a blob of modelling clay to one end.
3. Launch your 'flying ray' into the air. Adjust the tail weight until it glides smoothly.

Sharks need partners

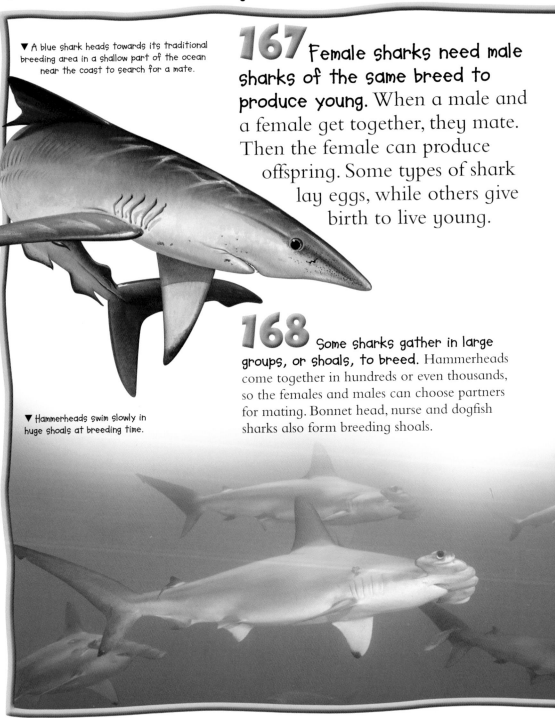

▼ A blue shark heads towards its traditional breeding area in a shallow part of the ocean near the coast to search for a mate.

167 **Female sharks need male sharks of the same breed to produce young.** When a male and a female get together, they mate. Then the female can produce offspring. Some types of shark lay eggs, while others give birth to live young.

168 **Some sharks gather in large groups, or shoals, to breed.** Hammerheads come together in hundreds or even thousands, so the females and males can choose partners for mating. Bonnet head, nurse and dogfish sharks also form breeding shoals.

▼ Hammerheads swim slowly in huge shoals at breeding time.

▼ Male white-tip reef sharks rest in the shallows, waiting for scents called pheromones to drift through the water, which tell them that females are nearby.

169 Sharks have a complicated way of getting together, known as courtship. They give off scents or 'perfumes' into the water to attract a partner. Then the two rub one another, wind their bodies around each other, and maybe even bite the other! The male may hold the female using his claspers, which are two long parts on his underside.

170 Some sharks don't breed very often. This can cause problems, especially when people catch too many of them. The sharks cannot breed fast enough to keep up their numbers, and they become rare and endangered.

Eggs and baby sharks

50 days

100 days

150 days

200 days

250 days

▲ A baby catshark develops slowly in its protective case. At 50 days it is smaller than its store of food, the yolk. It gradually develops and finally hatches eight months later.

I DON'T BELIEVE IT!

As the young of the sand tiger shark develop inside their mother, the bigger ones feed on the smaller ones.

171 **Some mother sharks lay eggs.** Each egg has a strong case with a developing baby shark, called an embryo, inside. The case has long threads, which stick to seaweed or rocks. Look out for empty egg cases on beaches. They are known as 'mermaids' purses'.

172 Some mother sharks do not lay eggs, but give birth to baby sharks, which are known as pups. The hammerhead and the basking shark do this. The pups have to look after themselves straight away. Shark parents do not care for their young.

▲ A lanternshark baby, or pup, still attached to its yolk, which continues to nourish its growth.

173 Some sharks have hundreds of babies at once! The whale shark may give birth to as many as 300 pups, each about 60 centimetres long.

174 Sadly, most young sharks die. The mothers lay eggs or give birth in sheltered places such as bays, inlets and reefs, where there are plenty of places to hide. But the young sharks are easy prey for hunters, such as dolphins, barracudas, sea lions – and other sharks.

▼ The egg cases of the Port Jackson shark are spiral-shaped. The mother picks up each egg in her mouth and wedges it into a safe place such as under a rock.

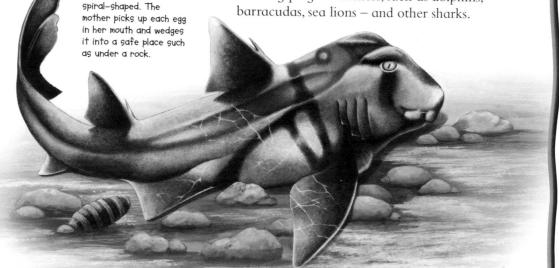

Sharks can 'disappear'

175 **Some sharks blend into their surroundings so well that they are hardly noticed.** This is called camouflage. The wobbegong has a lumpy body with blotches and frills that look just like rocks and seaweed. It waits for a fish to swim past, then opens its huge mouth to grab the victim.

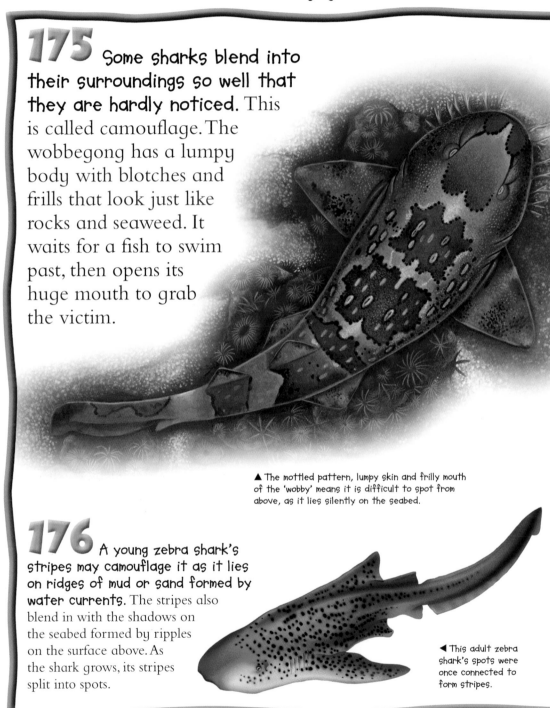

▲ The mottled pattern, lumpy skin and frilly mouth of the 'wobby' means it is difficult to spot from above, as it lies silently on the seabed.

176 **A young zebra shark's stripes may camouflage it as it lies on ridges of mud or sand formed by water currents.** The stripes also blend in with the shadows on the seabed formed by ripples on the surface above. As the shark grows, its stripes split into spots.

◀ This adult zebra shark's spots were once connected to form stripes.

177 Angel sharks have wide, flat bodies the same colour as sand. They blend perfectly into the sandy seabed as they lie in wait for prey. They are called 'angel' sharks because their fins spread wide like an angel's wings.

▶ The flattened body of the angel shark looks like a low lump in the sandy seabed.

178 Even in the open ocean, sharks can be hard to spot. This is because of the way they are coloured, known as countershading. The shark's back is darker while its underside is lighter. Seen from above the dark back blends in with the gloom of deeper water below. Seen from below the pale belly merges with the brighter water's surface and sky above.

▼ A side view of this silvertip shark shows countershading – darker back, lighter underside.

WHICH SHARKS LIVE WHERE?

Pair up these sharks and the habitats in which live.
1. Blue shark – light blue above, mainly white below
2. Wobbegong – green and brown blotches, lumps and frills
3. Spotted dogfish – dark blotches on light body

Habitats:
A. Sandy seabed
B. Open ocean
C. Rocks and weeds

Answers:
1 B
2 C 3 A

81

Shark friends

▼ Cleaner wrasse gather around the mouth and gill slits of this white-tip reef shark.

179 **Some fish enter a shark's mouth – and live!** These small, brightly coloured fish are called cleaner wrasse. The shark allows them to nibble off bits of skin, scales and pests such as sea leeches and barnacles, from its body, gills, mouth and teeth. The shark gets tidied up and has its teeth cleaned, and the cleaner fish have a good meal. A helpful relationship like this between two species of animal is called 'symbiosis'.

180 Some fish like to swim along very near to sharks. They are called pilotfish and often cluster just below and in front of the shark's mouth. They may feel safe from large predators that might eat them. They could be waiting for bits of food falling from the shark's mouth. Or they may be saving energy by swimming in the shark's slipstream – the swirls and currents made by its movement.

TRUE OR FALSE?
1. Fish that enter a shark's mouth are always eaten.
2. Remoras eat the scraps of food that sharks leave behind.
3. A helpful relationship between two different species of animal is called 'symbiosis'.

Answers:
1 False.
2 True. 3 True.

181 Some fish attach themselves to sharks and travel with them through the ocean. Remoras or sharksuckers have a ridged sucker on their heads. This clamps to the underside of a large shark (or other big sea creature). Using this, the remora saves energy by getting a free ride, and it can let go to feed on scraps from the shark's meal.

▼ This remora (below) has just detached from a bull shark, showing its sucker-topped head.

Sharks on the move

182 There are about 330 kinds of sharks, but only a few leave the salty water of the sea and swim into the fresh water of rivers. One is the bull shark, which travels hundreds of kilometres up rivers, especially in South America. It has attacked people fishing, washing or boating in lakes.

▼ Not all sharks travel far afield. The Galapagos shark stays close to home, swimming only in one small area.

183 The most common sharks are blue sharks, which are found in almost every part of every ocean except the icy polar seas. In the Atlantic Ocean, they travel from the Caribbean to Western Europe, down to Africa, and back to the Caribbean – 6000 kilometres in one year!

184 Some sharks live in small areas and rarely stray outside them. One is the Galapagos shark, which swims around a few small groups of mid-ocean islands in the tropics.

All epaulette sharks have a large black ocellus (an eye-like spot), above the pectoral fin

Large pectoral fins allow the epaulette shark to travel along the seabed

▲ One of the few sharks that regularly moves out of water is the epaulette shark. It drags itself between rock pools using its strong pectoral fins.

185 Epaulette sharks can leave the water and move over dry land. They can drag themselves along the seashore from one rock pool to the next by using their strong pectoral fins like 'arms'.

I DON'T BELIEVE IT!

Most submarines can't dive beyond 500 metres, but the Portuguese shark can swim over 3500 metres below the surface.

186 Sharks may have a built-in compass. People use magnetic compasses to find their way across the seas or remote lands. The compass detects the natural magnetism of the Earth and points north-south. Sharks may be able to detect the Earth's magnetism too, using tiny parts of their bodies. Other animals can do this too, such as certain birds and turtles. This could help sharks find their way across oceans.

Science and sharks

187 Scientists study sharks around the world – especially how they live, behave and travel. Small radio-transmitter trackers can be attached to big sharks and the radio signals show where the shark roams. Smaller sharks have little plastic tags with letters and numbers attached to their fins. If the shark is caught again, its code can be traced.

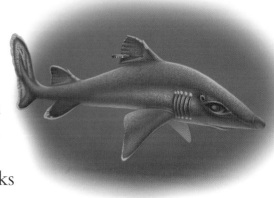

▲ This dogfish shark has a plastic tag fixed to its dorsal fin, so scientists can record its travels.

188 **Sharks show us problems in the oceans.** In some areas, sharks have disappeared for no obvious reason. This might suggest chemicals and pollution in the water, which upset the balance of nature. The chemicals could affect the sharks themselves, making them feel unwell so that they travel away. Or the pollution could affect the sharks' prey, such as small fish. Then the sharks have to hunt elsewhere for food.

▼ Huge aquariums let us watch the fascinating underwater world of sharks and other fish.

189 **Some sharks can live in captivity.** They are very popular with visitors to aquariums. People love to get up close to sharks and see their teeth, eyes, fins, and their grace and power as they swim. The captured animals can also help us to learn more about the species and how to protect them and their natural habitats.

190 **Sharks may help us to find new medicines.** Sharks seem to suffer from diseases and infections quite rarely compared to other animals. Scientists are examining their body parts, blood and the natural chemicals they produce in order to make better medical drugs for humans.

Shark attacks

191 **The most dangerous sharks include the great white, tiger and bull sharks.** However, a shark that attacks a person might not be properly identified. Attacks happen very quickly and the shark is soon gone. Some attacks blamed on great whites might well have been made by bull sharks instead.

▲ From below, a surfboard looks similar to a seal or a turtle, which may be the reason why large hunting sharks sometimes attack surfers.

▼ Great whites do sometimes attack humans, but their favourite foods are fish, seals and sea lions.

192 **Areas of the world known for shark attacks include the east coast of North America, the west coast of Africa and around Southeast Asia and Australia.** This is partly because these places are popular with swimmers and surfers.

193 Most shark attacks are not fatal. A shark may 'test-bite' a person and realize that this is not its usual prey. The victim may be injured, but not killed.

◀ Even quite large sharks are themselves hunted, by the huge elephant seal, which can weigh up to 5 tonnes.

194 The dangers of shark attacks can be reduced in many ways. Examples include shark barriers or nets around the beach, patrols by boats and planes, lookout towers, and only swimming in protected areas between flags.

▶ Movies about sharks often make them seem more eager to attack than in reality. The 1999 film *Deep Blue Sea* features blood-thirsty ultra-intelligent sharks.

195 Sharks do not attack people because they hate us. They are simply hungry and looking for a meal. They may sometimes mistake humans for their usual prey, such as sea lions.

I DON'T BELIEVE IT!

Each year there are less than ten fatal shark attacks — ten times less than the number of people killed by falling coconuts!

196 Sharks are not the most dangerous animals, by a long way! Each year, many more people are killed by poisonous snakes, tigers, elephants, hippos and crocodiles. Some tiny animals are much more lethal. Mosquitoes spread the disease malaria, which kills more than one million people every year.

Save our sharks

197 Some sharks have become very rare. They include the most feared of all, the great white. There are many reasons – hunting by people who think that all sharks are dangerous, sports angling where people use rods and lines to hook sharks, pollution, catching sharks for people to eat, and catching sharks by accident in nets meant for other fish such as tuna.

198 Sharks are made into many foods, including shark fin soup. Many other shark parts are eaten by people around the world, including the flesh as shark steaks, and the liver and other body parts in various oils, cosmetics and health foods. Sometimes, it's not obvious because names are changed. Meat from the small dogfish shark may be sold as 'rock salmon' or 'rock cod'.

▲ By getting very close to sharks, and studying their detailed behaviour, experts can help the conservation effort.

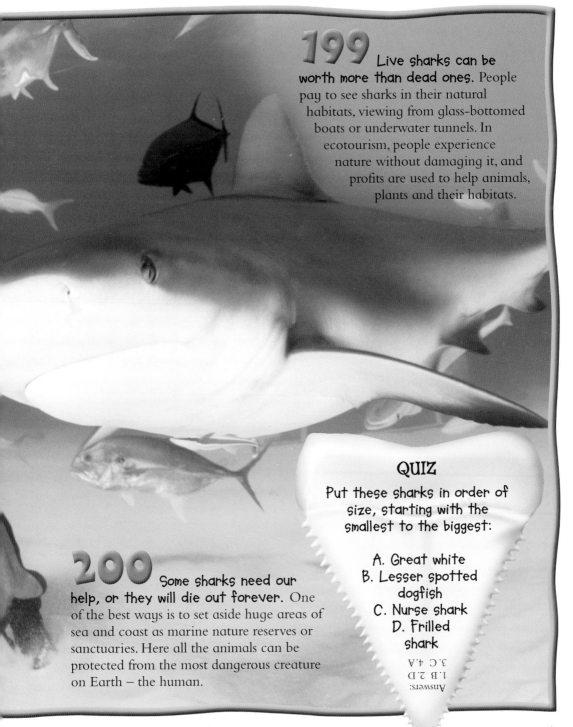

199 Live sharks can be worth more than dead ones. People pay to see sharks in their natural habitats, viewing from glass-bottomed boats or underwater tunnels. In ecotourism, people experience nature without damaging it, and profits are used to help animals, plants and their habitats.

QUIZ

Put these sharks in order of size, starting with the smallest to the biggest:

A. Great white
B. Lesser spotted dogfish
C. Nurse shark
D. Frilled shark

Answers:
1.B 2.D
3.C 4.A

200 Some sharks need our help, or they will die out forever. One of the best ways is to set aside huge areas of sea and coast as marine nature reserves or sanctuaries. Here all the animals can be protected from the most dangerous creature on Earth – the human.

Cold-blooded creatures

201 **Reptiles and amphibians are cold-blooded animals.** This means that they cannot control their body temperature like we can. A reptile's skin is dry and scaly, most reptiles spend much of their time on land. Most amphibians live in or around water. The skin of an amphibian is smooth and wet.

Nile crocodiles

Golden arrow-poison frog

Spotted salamander

Common frog

Eastern green
mamba snake

Komodo dragon

Jackson's
chameleon

Indian
cobra

Desert
tortoise

Frilled
lizard

Shingleback
lizard

93

Scales and slime

202 Reptiles and amphibians can be divided into smaller groups. There are four kinds of reptiles – snakes and lizards, the crocodile family, tortoises and turtles, and the tuatara. Amphibians are split into frogs and toads, newts and salamanders, and caecilians.

▲ Crocodiles are the largest reptiles in the world. Their eyes and nostrils are placed high on their heads so that they can stay mostly under water while approaching their prey.

203 Reptiles do a lot of sunbathing! They do this, called basking, to get themselves warm with the heat from the sun so that they can move about. When it gets cold, at night or during a cold season, they might sleep or hibernate, which means that they go into a very deep sleep.

204 Most reptiles have dry, scaly, waterproof skin. This stops their bodies from drying out. The scales are made of keratin and may form very thick, tough plates. Human nails are also made of the same sort of material.

▲ This reptile, an agama lizard from Africa, gets itself warm by lying, or basking, in the sun.

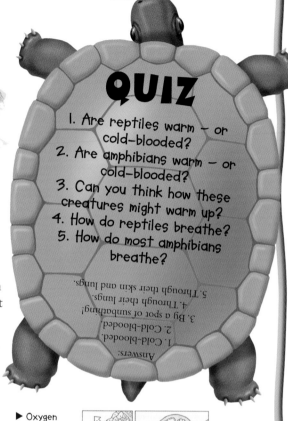

QUIZ

1. Are reptiles warm — or cold-blooded?
2. Are amphibians warm — or cold-blooded?
3. Can you think how these creatures might warm up?
4. How do reptiles breathe?
5. How do most amphibians breathe?

Answers:
1. Cold-blooded.
2. Cold-blooded.
3. By a spot of sunbathing!
4. Through their lungs.
5. Through their skin and lungs.

205 The average amphibian has skin that is moist, fairly smooth and soft. Oxygen can pass easily through their skin, which is important because most adult amphibians breathe through their skin as well as with their lungs. Reptiles breathe only through their lungs.

206 Amphibians' skin is kept moist by special glands just under the surface. These glands produce a sticky substance called mucus. Many amphibians also keep their skin moist by making sure that they are never far away from water.

► Oxygen passes in through the skin and into the blood, while carbon dioxide passes out.

Lung

207 Some amphibians have no lungs. Humans breathe with their lungs to get oxygen from the air and breathe out carbon dioxide. Most amphibians breathe through their skin and lungs, but lungless salamanders breathe only through their skin and the lining of the mouth.

Sun worshippers

208 Most reptiles live in warm or hot habitats. Many are found in dry, burning-hot places such as deserts and dry grassland. They have various clever ways of surviving in these harsh conditions.

Common iguana

209 Even reptiles can get too hot sometimes! When this happens, they hide in the shade of a rock or bury themselves in the sand. Some escape the heat by being nocturnal — coming out mostly at night.

Banded gecko

Desert tortoise

Spadefoot toad

210 Reptiles need very little food and water. Unlike warm-blooded animals, they don't use food to create body heat, so many can survive in places with scarce food supplies, such as deserts. Their thick skin means that as little water as possible escapes from their bodies.

211 Reptiles need a certain level of warmth to survive. This is why there are no reptiles in very cold places, such as at the North and South Poles, or at the very tops of mountains.

Banded gecko

Leopard lizard

Zebratail lizard

North American puff adder

212 Like reptiles, many amphibians live in very hot places. Sometimes it can get too hot and dry for them. The spadefoot toad from Europe, Asia and North America buries itself in the sand to escape the heat and dryness.

Cooler customers

213 Many amphibians are common in cooler, damper parts of the world. Amphibians like wet places. Most mate and lay their eggs in water.

214 As spring arrives, amphibians come out of hiding. The warmer weather sees many amphibians returning to the pond or stream where they were born. This may mean a very long journey through towns or over busy roads.

215 **When the weather turns especially cold, amphibians often hide away.** They simply hibernate in the mud at the bottom of ponds or under stones and logs. This means that they go to sleep in the autumn, and don't wake up until spring!

▶ This aquatic, or water-living, salamander is called a mudpuppy. It lives in freshwater lakes, rivers and streams in North America.

▲ The marbled newt of France and Italy is more colourful than most of its European relatives. Only juveniles and females have the vivid orange stripe along the spine. This species sometimes interbreeds with the great crested newt to produce hybrids.

216 **Journeys to breeding grounds may be up to 5 kilometres long, a long way for an animal only a few centimetres in length!** This is like a man walking to a pond 90 kilometres away without a map! The animals find their way by scent, landmarks, the Earth's magnetic field and the Sun's position.

Water babies

217 Amphibians live in water and on land. Most are born and grow up in fresh water such as ponds, pools, streams and rivers. They move onto dry land when they are adults and return to water to breed.

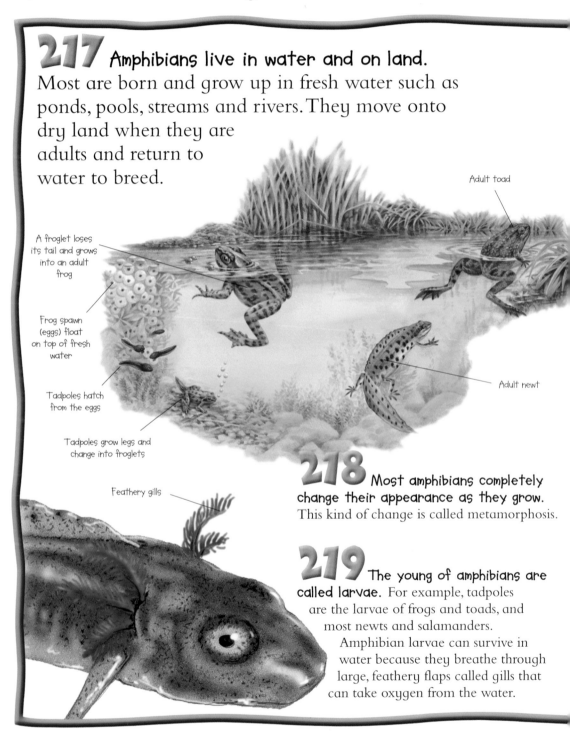

Adult toad

A froglet loses its tail and grows into an adult frog

Frog spawn (eggs) float on top of fresh water

Tadpoles hatch from the eggs

Tadpoles grow legs and change into froglets

Adult newt

Feathery gills

218 Most amphibians completely change their appearance as they grow. This kind of change is called metamorphosis.

219 The young of amphibians are called larvae. For example, tadpoles are the larvae of frogs and toads, and most newts and salamanders. Amphibian larvae can survive in water because they breathe through large, feathery flaps called gills that can take oxygen from the water.

▼ The axolotl lives only in Mexico, in the southern part of North America.

220 **The axolotl is an amphibian that has never grown up.** This type of water-living salamander has never developed beyond the larval stage. It does, however, develop far enough to be able to breed.

221 **The majority of amphibians lay soft eggs.** These may be in a jelly-like string or clump of tiny eggs called spawn, as with frogs and toads. Newts lay their eggs singly.

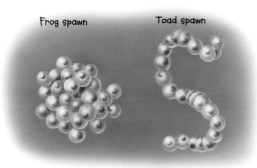

Frog spawn   Toad spawn

▲ Most amphibians lay their eggs in clumps or strings like these.

222 **A few amphibians give birth to live young instead of laying eggs.** The eggs of the fire salamander, for example, stay inside their mother, where the young hatch out and develop. She then gives birth to young that are like miniature adults.

Land babies

223 **The majority of reptiles spend their whole lives away from water.** They are very well adapted for life on dry land. Some do spend time in the water, but most reptiles lay their eggs on land.

▲ This female West African dwarf crocodile is laying her eggs in a hole, dug near to the water.

224 **Most reptile eggs are much tougher than those of amphibians.** This is because they must survive life out of the water. Lizards and snakes lay eggs with leathery shells. Crocodile and tortoise eggs have a hard shell rather like birds' eggs.

▲ Alligators lay their eggs in a mound of plants and earth. They lay between 35 and 40 eggs.

▲ A ground python's egg is large compared to its body. A female is about 85 centimetres long, and her eggs are about 12 centimetres long.

▲ A lizard called a Javan bloodsucker lays strange eggs like this. No one knows why their eggs are this very long thin shape.

▲ Galapagos giant tortoises lay round eggs like this one. They will hatch up to 200 days after they were laid.

225 **The eggs feed and protect the young developing inside them.** The egg yolk provides food for the developing young, called an embryo. The shell protects the embryo from the outside world, but also allows vital oxygen into the egg.

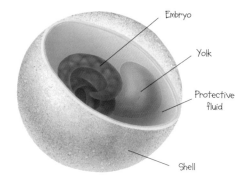

Embryo

Yolk

Protective fluid

Shell

INVESTIGATING EGGS

Reptile eggs are rather like birds' eggs. Next time you eat an omelette or boiled egg, rinse out half an empty eggshell, fill it with water, and wait a while. Do you see how no water escapes? Wash your hands well once you're done. Like this bird's eggshell, reptile eggshells stop the egg from drying out, although they let air in and are tough enough to protect the embryo.

226 **Young reptiles hatch out of eggs as miniature adults.** They do not undergo a change, or metamorphosis, like amphibians do.

▼ A baby reptile, such as this Burmese python, uses a sharp lump on the end of its snout to cut its way out of the egg. This 'egg tooth' falls off soon after the animal has hatched.

◄ Slow worms are not worms at all. They are legless lizards that live in Europe, Africa and Asia.

227 **Some snakes and lizards, like slow worms, don't lay eggs.** Instead, they give birth to fully developed live young. Animals that do this are called 'viviparous'.

Little and large

228 **Reptiles and amphibians come in every shape and size.** There are more than 6500 species (types) of reptiles and 4000 species of amphibians. They range from tiny frogs to giant, dinosaur-like lizards.

229 **The largest reptile award goes to the saltwater crocodile from around the Indian and west Pacific Oceans.** It measures a staggering 8 metres from nose to tail – an average adult man is not even 2 metres tall! Cold streams in Japan are home to the largest amphibian – a giant salamander that is around 1.5 metres long, and weighs up to 40 kilograms.

▲ The saltwater or estuarine crocodile lives in southern India, Indonesia and North Australia. It is the largest and one of the most dangerous species of crocodile.

▲ The giant salamander is mostly harmless and feeds on snails and worms.

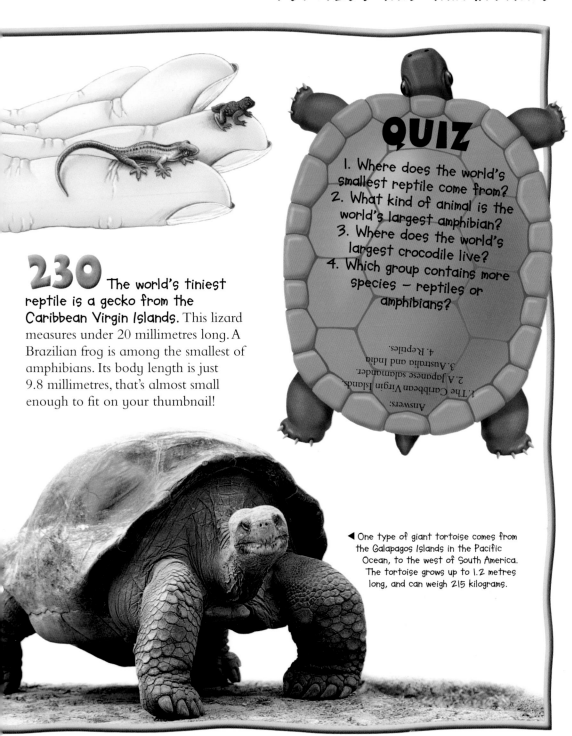

230
The world's tiniest reptile is a gecko from the Caribbean Virgin Islands. This lizard measures under 20 millimetres long. A Brazilian frog is among the smallest of amphibians. Its body length is just 9.8 millimetres, that's almost small enough to fit on your thumbnail!

QUIZ

1. Where does the world's smallest reptile come from?
2. What kind of animal is the world's largest amphibian?
3. Where does the world's largest crocodile live?
4. Which group contains more species – reptiles or amphibians?

Answers:
1. The Caribbean Virgin Islands
2. A Japanese salamander,
3. Australia and India
4. Reptiles.

◀ One type of giant tortoise comes from the Galapagos Islands in the Pacific Ocean, to the west of South America. The tortoise grows up to 1.2 metres long, and can weigh 215 kilograms.

Adaptable animals

231 **Many species have amazing special adaptations to help them live safely and easily in their surroundings.** Crocodiles, for example, have a special flap in their throats which means that they can open their mouth underwater without breathing in water.

232 **Geckos can climb up vertical surfaces or even upside down.** They are able to cling on because they have five wide-spreading toes, each with sticky toe-pads, on each foot. These strong pads are covered with millions of tiny hairs that grip surfaces tightly.

Wide toe-pads covered with tiny hairs

► A tokay gecko from South and Southeast Asia. It is one of the most common geckos, and also one of the largest, measuring up to 28 centimetres long. Tokay geckos are usually easy to find because they like to live around houses. The people of Asia and Indonesia believe that it is good luck for a gecko to come and live by or in their house!

233 **Tortoises and turtles have hard, bony shells for protection.** They form a suit of armour that protects them from predators (animals who might hunt and eat them) and also from the hot sun.

California newt

234 **Chameleons have adapted very well to their way of life in the trees.** They have long toes which can grip branches firmly, and a long tail that can grip branches like another hand. Tails that can grip like this are called 'prehensile'. Chameleons are also famous for being able to change their colour to blend in with their surroundings. This is called 'camouflage', and is something that many other reptiles and amphibians use.

235 **The flattened tails of newts make them expert swimmers.** Newts are salamanders that spend most of their lives in water, so they need to be able to get about speedily in this environment.

Gill

▶ This is a close-up view of a small part of a gill. As water flows over the gills, oxygen can pass into the amphibian's blood.

Water flows over the gills

READING ABOUT REPTILES

Pick a favourite reptile or amphibian and then find out as much as you can about it. List all the ways you think it is especially well adapted to deal with its lifestyle and habitat.

236 **An amphibian's gills enable it to breathe underwater.** Blood flows inside the feathery gills, at the same time as water flows over the outside. As the water flows past the gills, oxygen passes out of the water, straight into the blood of the amphibian.

Natural show-offs

▶ Cobras make themselves look more threatening by forming a wide hood of loose skin, stretched over flexible ribs.

237 Certain reptiles and amphibians love to make a show of themselves. Some of this 'display' behaviour is used to attract females when the breeding season comes around. It is also used to make enemies think twice before attacking.

238 Male newts go to great lengths to impress during the mating season. Great crested newts develop frills along their backs, black spots over their skin, and a red flush across the breast. Their colourful spring coat also warns off enemies.

▲ This great crested newt from Europe is showing its colours.

239 The male anole lizard of Central and South America guards his territory and mates jealously. When rival males come too close, he puffs out a bright red throat pouch at them. Two males may face each other with inflated throats for hours at a time!

Common toad

Throat pouch

240 Many frogs and toads also puff themselves up. Toads can inflate their bodies to look more frightening. Frogs and toads can puff out their throat pouches. This makes their croaking love-calls to mates, and 'back off' calls to enemies, much louder.

241 A frilled lizard in full display is an amazing sight. This lizard has a large flap of neck skin that normally lies flat. When faced by a predator, it spreads this out to form a huge, stiff ruff that makes it look bigger and scarier!

242 Male monitor lizards have their own wrestling competitions! At the beginning of the mating season they compete to try to win the females. They rear up on their hind legs and wrestle until the weaker animal gives up.

◀ The frilled lizard lives in Australia and New Guinea. Its frill can be up to 25 centimetres across, almost half the length of its body!

Sensitive creatures

243 Reptiles and amphibians find out about the world by using their senses such as sight, smell and touch. Some animals have lost senses that they don't need. Worm-like amphibians called caecilians, for example, spend their whole lives underground, so they don't have any use for eyes. However, some animals have developed new senses that are very unusual!

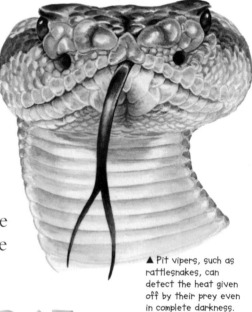

▲ Pit vipers, such as rattlesnakes, can detect the heat given off by their prey even in complete darkness.

244 Frogs and toads have developed new senses. They have something called Jacobson's organ in the roofs of their mouths. This helps them to 'taste' and 'smell' the outside world. Jacobson's organ is also found in snakes and some lizards.

245 Snakes have poor hearing and eyesight but they make up for it in other ways. They can find prey by picking up its vibrations travelling through the ground. Some snakes have pits in their faces that detect heat given off by prey. In contrast to snakes, frogs and toads have large and well-developed eardrums and very good hearing.

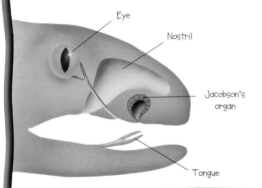

Eye

Nostril

Jacobson's organ

Tongue

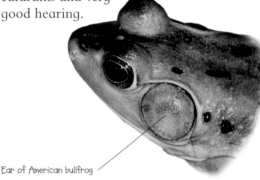

Ear of American bullfrog

▼ The Fijian banded iguana lives on the islands of Fiji and Tonga in the Pacific Ocean.

I DON'T BELIEVE IT!

One African gecko has such thin skin over its ear-openings that if you were to look at it with the openings lined up precisely, you would see light coming through from the other side of its head!

246 Geckos and iguanas have large eyes and very good eyesight. They are a type of lizard that can't blink. Instead of having movable eyelids like humans, they have fixed, transparent 'spectacles' over their eyes. Most lizards have very good sight – they need it to hunt down their small and fast insect prey.

Large eyes give the gecko excellent vision.

Geckos lick their eyes to keep them clean.

▲ This is a web-footed gecko from southwest Africa. It lives in the Namib Desert, where it hardly ever rains. To get the water it needs, it licks dew from the stones, and also licks its own eyes!

Expert hunters

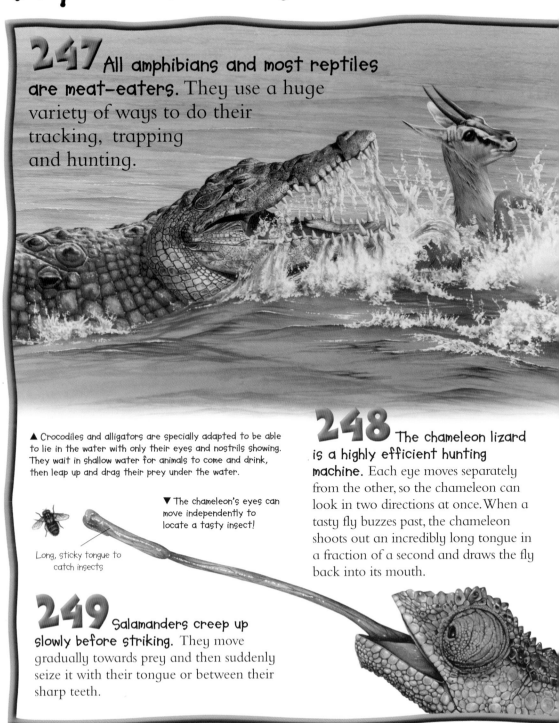

247 **All amphibians and most reptiles are meat-eaters.** They use a huge variety of ways to do their tracking, trapping and hunting.

▲ Crocodiles and alligators are specially adapted to be able to lie in the water with only their eyes and nostrils showing. They wait in shallow water for animals to come and drink, then leap up and drag their prey under the water.

▼ The chameleon's eyes can move independently to locate a tasty insect!

Long, sticky tongue to catch insects

248 **The chameleon lizard is a highly efficient hunting machine.** Each eye moves separately from the other, so the chameleon can look in two directions at once. When a tasty fly buzzes past, the chameleon shoots out an incredibly long tongue in a fraction of a second and draws the fly back into its mouth.

249 **Salamanders creep up slowly before striking.** They move gradually towards prey and then suddenly seize it with their tongue or between their sharp teeth.

250

Crocodiles and snakes can open their fierce jaws extra wide to eat huge dinners! A snake can separate its jaw bones to eat huge eggs or to gulp down animals much larger than its head. A large snake can swallow pigs and deer – whole!

BE A CHAMELEON!

Like a chameleon, you need two eyes to judge distances easily. Here's an experiment to prove it!

Close one eye. Hold a finger out in front of you, and with one eye open, try to touch this fingertip with the other. It's not as easy as it looks! Now open both eyes and you'll find it a lot easier!

Two eyes give your brain two slightly different angles to look at the object, so it is easier to tell how far away it is!

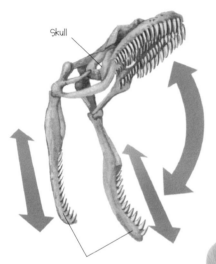

Skull

A snake's lower jaws can work separately. First one side pulls, and then the other, to draw the prey into the throat

The snake's lower jaws can detach from its skull to eat large prey

251

A snake has to swallow things whole. This is because it has no large back teeth for crushing prey and can't chew.

▶ Snakes kill their prey with a lethal bite. Then they swallow the victim, such as a rodent, whole.

Fliers and leapers

252 Some reptiles and amphibians can take to the air — if only for a few seconds. This helps animals to travel further, escape predators or swoop down on passing prey before it gets away.

254 Even certain kinds of snake can glide. The flying snake lives in the tropical forests of southern Asia. It can jump between branches or glide through the air in 'S' movements.

◄ Flying snakes can glide between branches of trees to hunt lizards and frogs.

► The flying dragon lizard has taken things a step further than the geckos. Its 'wings' are skin stretched out over ribs that can even fold back when they are not in use!

◄ Flying geckos' skills are all important for food. Either they are trying to catch food, or they are trying to avoid becoming food for something else!

253 Gliding snakes fly by making their bodies into parachutes. They do this by raising their ribcages so that their bodies flatten out like a ribbon.

255 Flying geckos form another group of natural parachutes. They have webbed feet and folds of skin along their legs, tail and sides, which together form the perfect gliding machine.

256 Some frogs can glide.

Deep in the steamy rainforests of southeast Asia and South America, tree frogs flit from tree to tree. Some can glide as far as 12 metres, clinging to their landing spot with suckers on their feet.

257 Frogs and toads use their powerful hind legs for hopping or jumping.

The greatest frog leaper comes from Africa. Known as the rocket frog, it has been known to jump up to 4.2 metres.

FLYING FROGS!

See frogs fly through the air with the greatest of ease by making your own frog bean bags!

1. Ask an adult to help you. Cut out two triangle shapes of green material.

2. Sew the edges together, but leave one end free.

3. Turn the frog inside out and fill him up with dried beans. Now sew up the end.

4. Finally, draw on your frog's legs and eyes. Now make your frog a friend and you're ready to go!

1. The powerful muscles in the frog's hind legs push off.

2. In mid-leap, the frog's hind legs are fully stretched out, its front legs are held back, and its eyes are closed for protection.

3. As it lands, its body arches and the front legs act as a brake.

Slitherers and crawlers

258 Most reptiles, and some amphibians, spend much of their time creeping, crawling and slithering along the ground. In fact, scientists call the study of reptiles and amphibians 'herpetology', which comes from a Greek word meaning 'to creep or crawl'.

▲ The sidewinding viper lives in the deserts of the United States. It moves by pushing its body sideways against the sand which leaves a series of marks shaped like sideways letter 'J's.

259 A snake's skin does not grow with its body. This means that it has to shed its skin to grow bigger. This grass snake from Europe is slithering right out of its old skin!

260 Some frogs and toads also shed their skin. The European toad sheds its skin several times during the summer – and then eats it! This recycles the goodness in the toad's skin.

261 Snakes and caecilians have no legs.

Caecilians are amphibians that look like worms or snakes. They move around by slithering about gracefully. Small snakes have about 180 vertebrae, or backbones. Large snakes can have 400! They have very strong muscles to enable them to move, so their backbones are also extra strong to stand up to the strain.

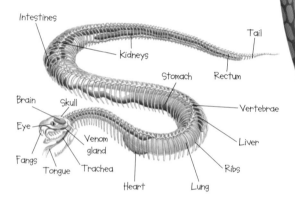

Intestines
Tail
Kidneys
Stomach
Rectum
Brain
Skull
Eye
Venom gland
Vertebrae
Fangs
Liver
Tongue
Trachea
Ribs
Heart
Lung

262 A ground snake has special scales on the underside of its body.

These help it to grip the ground as it moves along.

▶ The scales on the underside of some snakes overlap. This helps it moves smoothly, and also provides the snake with more grip.

SLITHER AND SLIDE!

Make your own slithery snake. First you need to collect as many cotton reels as you can, and paint them lots of bright colours. Next, cut a forked tongue and some snake eyes out of some paper and stick them onto one of the reels to make a head. Now, just thread your reels onto a piece of string. Make sure you don't put the head in the middle!

263 Some reptiles and amphibians slither below the surface.

In hot, desert-like places, snakes burrow down into the sand to escape the sun's fierce heat. Caecilians' heads are perfectly shaped to burrow through the mud of their tropical homelands, searching for worms.

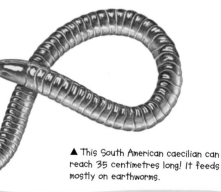

▲ This South American caecilian can reach 35 centimetres long! It feeds mostly on earthworms.

Fast and slow

264 The reptile and amphibian worlds contain their fair share of fast and slow movers. But the slow-coaches are not necessarily at a disadvantage. A predator may be able to seize the slow-moving tortoise, but it certainly can't bite through its armour-plated shell!

▶ The sidewinder snake moves at up to 4 kilometres per hour over the shifting sands of its desert home.

265 Tortoises never take life in a hurry and are among the slowest animals on Earth. The top speed for a giant tortoise is 5 metres per minute! These giant tortoises live on the small Galapagos islands in the Pacific Ocean, and not anywhere else in the world.

266 Chameleons are also slow-movers. They move slowly through the trees, barely noticeable as they hunt for insects.

▲ The giant tortoise is definitely a slow mover at only 0.3 kilometres per hour!

▲ The chameleon is a very slow mover, until its tongue pops out to trap a passing fly!

▶ Tuataras live on a few small islands off the coast of New Zealand.

267
Some lizards can trot off at high speed by 'standing up'. Water dragon lizards from Asia can simply rear up onto their hind legs to make a dash for it – much faster than moving on four legs.

◀ The speedy crested water dragon can run on its back legs to escape predators.

268
One of the world's slowest animals is the lizard-like tuatara. When resting, it breathes just once an hour, and may still be growing when it is 60 years old! Their slow lifestyle in part means that they can live to be 120 years old! The tuatara is sometimes called a 'living fossil'. This is because it is the only living species of a group of animals that died out millions of years ago. No one knows why only the tuatara survives.

FLAT RACE

Get together a group of friends and hold your own animal race day. Each of you cuts a flat animal shape – a frog or tortoise, say – out of paper or very light card. If you wish, add details with coloured pencils or pens. Now race your animals along the ground to the finishing line by flapping a newspaper or a magazine behind them.

269
Racerunner lizards, from North and South America, are true to their name. The six-lined racerunner is the fastest recorded reptile on land. In 1941 in South Carolina, USA it was recorded reaching an amazing speed of 29 kilometres per hour!

◀ The six-lined racerunner from America is the fastest reptile on land.

Champion swimmers

270 Amphibians are well known for their links with water, but some types of reptile are also aquatic (live in the water). Different types of amphibian and reptile have developed all kinds of ways of tackling watery lifestyles.

Hellbender

Rough-skinned newt

Eastern newt

271 Newts and salamanders swim rather like fish. They make an 'S'-shape as they move. Many have flat tails that help to propel them along in the water.

272 Toads and frogs propel themselves by kicking back with their hind legs. They use their front legs as a brake for landing when they dive into the water. Large, webbed feet act like flippers, helping them to push through the water.

1. Frog draws its legs up

2. Pushes its feet out to the side

3. The main kick back with toes spread propels the frog forward through the water

4. Frog closes its toes and draws its legs in and up for the next kick

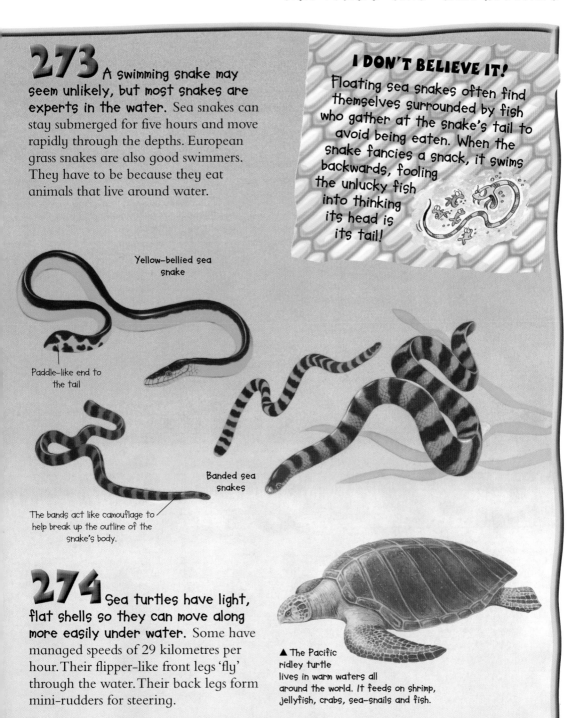

273 **A swimming snake may seem unlikely, but most snakes are experts in the water.** Sea snakes can stay submerged for five hours and move rapidly through the depths. European grass snakes are also good swimmers. They have to be because they eat animals that live around water.

I DON'T BELIEVE IT!

Floating sea snakes often find themselves surrounded by fish who gather at the snake's tail to avoid being eaten. When the snake fancies a snack, it swims backwards, fooling the unlucky fish into thinking its head is its tail!

Yellow-bellied sea snake

Paddle-like end to the tail

Banded sea snakes

The bands act like camouflage to help break up the outline of the snake's body.

274 **Sea turtles have light, flat shells so they can move along more easily under water.** Some have managed speeds of 29 kilometres per hour. Their flipper-like front legs 'fly' through the water. Their back legs form mini-rudders for steering.

▲ The Pacific ridley turtle lives in warm waters all around the world. It feeds on shrimp, jellyfish, crabs, sea-snails and fish.

Nature's tanks

275 Tortoises and turtles are like armoured tanks – slow but very well-protected by their shells. Tortoises live on land and eat mainly plants. Some turtles are flesh-eaters that live in the salty sea. Other turtles, some of which are called terrapins, live in freshwater lakes and rivers.

276 When danger threatens, tortoises can quickly retreat into their mobile homes. They simply draw their head, tail and legs into their shell.

277 Tortoises and turtles are ancient members of the reptile world. They are the oldest living reptiles, and might have been around with the very first dinosaurs, about 200 million years ago. They also live longer than almost any other animal – some for up to 150 years!

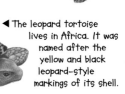

▶ The matamata turtle lives only in South America. It is one of the strangest of all turtles, as its head is almost flat, and is shaped like a triangle. It lies on the bottom of rivers and eats fish that swim past.

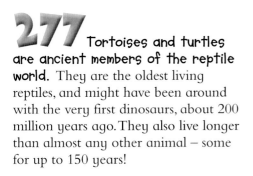

▶ The Indian softshell turtle is also called the narrow-headed turtle because of its long, thin head. It is a very fast swimmer that feeds on fish.

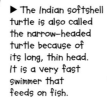

◀ The leopard tortoise lives in Africa. It was named after the yellow and black leopard-style markings of its shell.

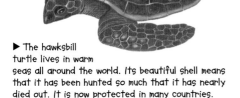

▶ The hawksbill turtle lives in warm seas all around the world. Its beautiful shell means that it has been hunted so much that it has nearly died out. It is now protected in many countries.

278 Some sea turtles are among nature's greatest travellers. The green turtle migrates an amazing 2000 kilometres from its feeding grounds off the coast of Brazil to breeding sites such as Ascension Island, in the South Atlantic.

Green turtle

Dangerous enemies

279 **Animals such as crocodiles, some snakes and snapping turtles make nasty enemies.** Snakes are famed for poisoning or strangling prey before gobbling it down. Other reptiles have also found ways of making themselves especially dangerous.

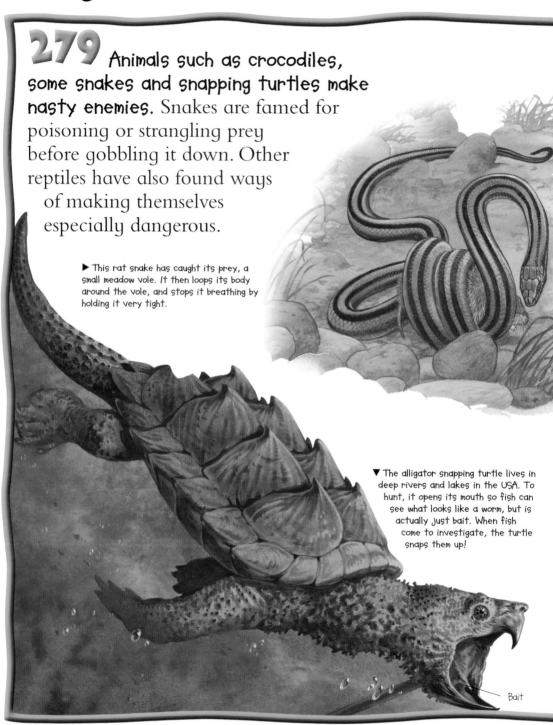

► This rat snake has caught its prey, a small meadow vole. It then loops its body around the vole, and stops it breathing by holding it very tight.

▼ The alligator snapping turtle lives in deep rivers and lakes in the USA. To hunt, it opens its mouth so fish can see what looks like a worm, but is actually just bait. When fish come to investigate, the turtle snaps them up!

Bait

Venom gland

Folding fangs

Tube for venom to be injected

280 **Poisonous snakes inject venom (poison) into their prey.** They do this through grooved or hollow teeth called fangs. Rattlesnakes are poisonous snakes with a rattle at the end of their tail that they shake to frighten predators. Constricting snakes such as pythons coil themselves around victims and squeeze them to death.

▼ The tiger salamander comes from North America. It is the largest land-living salamander in the world, growing up to 40 centimetres long.

▼ The gila monster from the desert areas of North America is one of only two venomous lizards in the world. The gila stores fat in its tail, to live off when it can't find food.

▶ The strawberry poison-dart frog is also known as the 'blue jeans' frog because of its blue legs.

281 Bright patterns on some amphibians' skin warn predators. Their skin may be foul-tasting or causes irritation. Arrow-poison frogs from South America's rainforests have very bright colours, while fire salamanders have bright yellow spots or stripes.

Clever mimics

282 From crocodiles and tortoises to lizards and frogs, reptiles and amphibians are masters of disguise. Some blend into their surroundings naturally, while others can change their appearance – perfect for avoiding predators or sneaking up on prey.

Green tree frog

Arum lily frog

Malaysian horned frog

Natal ghost frog

283 Frogs and toads are experts in the art of camouflage (blending with surroundings). Many are coloured shades of green or green-brown, to look just like leaves, grass or tree bark.

African clawed toad

Frilled leaf-tailed gecko

284 Many lizards have green or brown camouflage colouring, too. The chameleon lizard can also change its colour. If it meets an enemy whilst it is walking along a branch, it can stay very still, crouch down and make itself look like the leaves and bark.

287 **The fire-bellied toad has a bright red tummy!** It uses it to distract its enemies. When it's threatened it leaps away to safety, and the quick flash of bright red confuses the attacker, and gives the frog an extra fraction of a second to escape.

▲ The fire-bellied toad has a bright red stomach, which it uses to distract predators. When threatened, the toad leaps away, exposing its belly. The quick flash of bright red confuses the attacker, giving the toad an extra fraction of a second to make its escape.

▼ This European grass snake is pretending to be dead. It rolls over onto its back, wiggles as if dying, and then lies still with its mouth open and its tongue hanging out!

285 **Some snakes can even pretend to be dead.** They lie coiled up with their tongue hanging out, so that predators will look elsewhere for a meal.

286 **The alligator snapper looks like a rough rock as it lies on the ocean floor.** This cunning turtle has an extra trick up its sleeve. The tip of its tongue looks like a juicy worm, which it waves at passing prey to lure them into its jaws.

ANIMAL DISGUISE!

Make a mask of your favourite reptile or amphibian from a piece of card or a paper plate. Attach some string or elastic to hold it to your head, cut some eye-holes and then colour it all in. You could also try making felt finger puppets – and have a whole handful of reptiles!

Escape artists

288 Reptiles and amphibians form food for other animals. They have developed clever ways to escape predators and survive – at least long enough to grow up and breed.

289 Some salamanders and lizards have detachable tails. If a predator grabs a five-lined tree skink lizard by the tail, it will be left just holding a twitching blue tail! The tail does grow back.

290 The chuckwalla lizard gets itself into tight corners. It can jam itself into a rock crevice, then puff its body up so that predators cannot pull it out.

291
A young blue-tongued skink uses colour as a delay tactic. The lizard simply flashes its bright blue tongue and mouth lining at enemies. The startled predator lets its prey slip away.

I DON'T BELIEVE IT!
The Jesus Christ lizard is named because it can sprint at high speed across the surface of water on its hind legs!

292
The Australian shingleback lizard has a tail shaped like a head. By the time a confused predator has worked this one out, the lizard has made its getaway.

▲ The shingleback lizard, which end is its head?

293
Crocodiles can walk on their tails! If they are being threatened they can move so fast they almost leap out of the water! This is called 'tail-walking'.

Close relatives

294 **An alligator isn't quite the same as a crocodile and a frog isn't quite the same as a toad.** These pairs of animals are very similar, but they do have certain differences. If you look carefully, you will be able to spot the small differences between them.

▼ This Nile crocodile lives in Africa. It eats large mammals and birds which it catches from the water's edge while they drink.

Pointed snout

Tooth showing

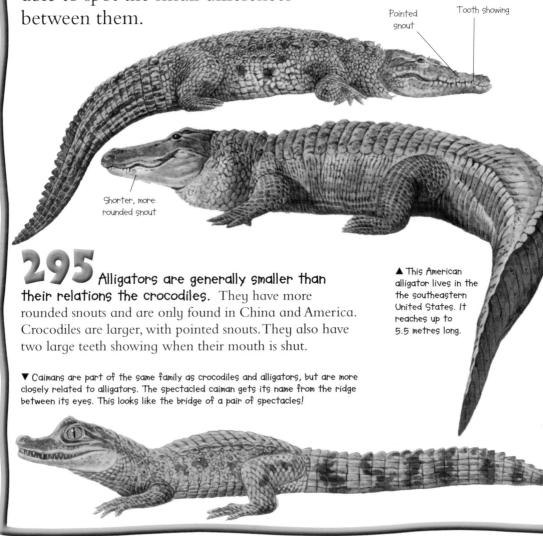

Shorter, more rounded snout

295 **Alligators are generally smaller than their relations the crocodiles.** They have more rounded snouts and are only found in China and America. Crocodiles are larger, with pointed snouts. They also have two large teeth showing when their mouth is shut.

▲ This American alligator lives in the the southeastern United States. It reaches up to 5.5 metres long.

▼ Caimans are part of the same family as crocodiles and alligators, but are more closely related to alligators. The spectacled caiman gets its name from the ridge between its eyes. This looks like the bridge of a pair of spectacles!

296
Crocodiles and alligators also have some other, very special and rather surprising close relations. They are the closest living relatives of the dinosaurs! The dinosaurs were also reptiles that lived millions of years ago. No one knows why, but all of the dinosaurs died out about 65 million years ago. For some reason, certain other animals that were also around at this time, like crocodiles, alligators and also turtles, survived.

I DON'T BELIEVE IT!
Whether a baby alligator is a girl or boy depends on temperature. A boy will develop in a warm egg, but a girl will develop in a cold one. For crocodiles, it's the other way around!

Short skull

Long legs will become shorter as Protosuchus evolves

▼ Protosuchus is one of the ancestors of the crocodiles. It lived about 225 million years ago during the Triassic Period. It had quite a short skull, which shows that it had not yet adapted fully for eating fish. It probably ate small lizards.

297
Most frogs live in damp places. Their bodies suit this environment. They tend to have strongly webbed feet, long back legs and smooth skin.

Tree frog

298
Most toads spend their time on dry land. They don't have strongly webbed feet and their skin is warty and quite dry. Toads are normally shorter and squatter than frogs, with shorter legs.

African bullfrog

Scary monsters

299 Early explorers told amazing tales of dragons living in faraway lands that few people had visited. It may be that these explorers had somehow seen flying lizards or giant monitor lizards such as the Komodo dragon. Perhaps this is how myths about dragons started.

Komodo dragon

Gould's monitor lizard

Flying dragon

Nile monitor lizard

300 Monitor lizards are long-necked reptiles from Australia, Asia and Africa. The rare Komodo dragon is a monitor from a group of islands in Indonesia, southeast Asia. It is the largest, fiercest lizard alive, up to 4 metres long, weighing 140 kilograms and eating small deer and wild boar.

What are birds?

301 A bird has two legs, a pair of wings and a body that is covered with feathers. Birds are, perhaps, the animals we see most often in the wild. They live all over the world – everywhere from Antarctica to the hottest deserts and rainforests. They range in size from the huge ostrich, which stands 2.75 metres tall, a whole metre taller than a man, to the tiny bee hummingbird, which is scarcely bigger than a real bee.

Osprey

Greater flamingo

Grey heron

Mallard

Kingfisher

Greater
honeyguide

Helmeted
hornbill

Masai
ostrich

Red-billed
hornbill

Lesser
green
broadbill

African
Jacana

Blue
peafowl

Blue-crowned
hanging parrot

The bird world

302 There are more than 9000 different types, or species, of bird. These have been organized by scientists into groups called orders which contain many different species. The largest order is called the passerines, also known as perching or songbirds. These include common birds such as robins.

Crown
Bill, or beak
Throat
Lung
Heart
Liver
Flight feathers
Light, hollow bones, or skeleton
Kidney
Stomach
Tail feathers
Toes

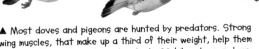

▲ Most doves and pigeons are hunted by predators. Strong wing muscles, that make up a third of their weight, help them to take off rapidly and accelerate to 80 kilometres an hour.

303 Birds are the only creatures that have feathers. The feathers are made of keratin – the same material as our hair and nails. Feathers keep a bird warm and protect it from the wind and rain. Its wing and tail feathers allow a bird to fly. Some birds also have very colourful feathers which help them to attract mates or blend in with their surroundings. This is called camouflage.

▶ The bird with the most feathers is thought to be the whistling swan, with more than 25,000 feathers.

304 All birds have wings. These are the bird's front limbs. There are many different wing shapes. Birds that soar in the sky for hours, such as hawks and eagles, have long broad wings. These allow them to make the best use of air currents. Small fast-flying birds such as swifts have slim, pointed wings.

▶ The egg protects the growing young and provides it with food. While the young develops the parent birds, such as this song thrush, keep the egg safe and warm.

305

All birds lay eggs. It would be impossible for birds to carry their developing young inside their bodies like mammals do – they would become too heavy to fly.

306

All birds have a beak for eating. The beak is made of bone and is covered with a hard material called horn. Birds have different kinds of beak for different types of food. Insect-eating birds tend to have thin, sharp beaks for picking up their tiny prey. The short, strong parrot's beak is ideal for cracking hard-shelled nuts.

QUIZ

1. How many types of bird are there?
2. How many feathers does the whistling swan have?
3. What are feathers made of?
4. What is the largest order of birds called?
5. What sort of beaks do hunting birds have?

Answers:
1. More than 9000
2. More than 25,000 3. Keratin
4. The passerines 5. Powerful hooked beaks

◀ Hunting birds, such as this goshawk, have powerful hooked beaks for tearing flesh.

Big and small

307 **The world's largest bird is the ostrich.** This long-legged bird stands up to 2.75 metres tall and weighs up to 115 kilograms – twice as much as an average adult human. Males are slightly larger than females. The ostrich lives on the grasslands of Africa where it feeds on plant material such as leaves, flowers and seeds.

▼ The great bustard lives in southern Europe and parts of Asia.

308 **The heaviest flying bird is the great bustard.** The male is up to 1 metre long and weighs about 18 kilograms, although the female is slightly smaller. The bustard is a strong flier, but it does spend much of its life on the ground, walking or running on its strong legs.

Bee hummingbird

309 **The bee hummingbird is the world's smallest bird.** Its body, including its tail, is only about 5 centimetres long and it weighs only 2 grams – about the same as a small spoonful of rice. It lives on Caribbean islands and, like other hummingbirds, feeds on flower nectar.

310 **The largest bird of prey is the Andean condor.** A type of vulture, this bird measures about 110 centimetres long and weighs up to 12 kilograms. This huge bird of prey soars over the Andes Mountains of South America, hunting for food.

▼ Like most vultures, the condor is a scavenger. It looks for carrion, the carcasses of dead animals and the remains of other hunters' kills.

◄ The wandering albatross only comes to land at breeding time. It lays its eggs on islands in the South Pacific, South Atlantic and Indian Ocean.

QUIZ

1. How much does a bee hummingbird weigh?
2. Where do ostriches live?
3. What does the great bustard eat?
4. How long are the wandering albatross's wings?
5. Where does the collared falconet live?

Answers:
1. 2 grams 2. Africa 3. Insects and seeds 4. 3.3 metres from tip to tip 5. India and Southeast Asia

311 The wandering albatross has the longest wings of any bird. When outstretched, they measure as much as 3.3 metres from tip to tip. The albatross spends most of its life in the air. It flies over the oceans, searching for fish and squid which it snatches from the water surface.

312 Wilson's storm petrel is the smallest seabird in the world. Only 16 to 19 centimetres long, this petrel hops over the water surface snatching up tiny sea creatures to eat. It is very common over the Atlantic, Indian and Antarctic Oceans.

313 The smallest bird of prey is the collared falconet. This little bird, which lives in India and Southeast Asia, is only about 19 centimetres long. It hunts insects and other small birds.

Fast movers

314 **The fastest flying bird is the peregrine falcon.** It hunts other birds in the air and makes spectacular high-speed dives to catch its prey. During a hunting dive, a peregrine may move as fast as 180 kilometres an hour. In normal level flight, it flies at about 95 kilometres an hour. Peregrine falcons live almost all over the world.

▲ The peregrine falcon does not just fold its wings and fall like many birds, it actually pushes itself down towards the ground. This powered dive is called a stoop.

315 **Ducks and geese are also fast fliers.** Many of them can fly at speeds of more than 65 kilometres an hour. The red-breasted merganser and the common eider duck can fly at up to 100 kilometres an hour.

Sword-billed hummingbird

When this hummingbird lands, it has to tilt its head right back to support the weight of its huge bill

Tail feathers spread for landing

316 **A hummingbird's wings beat 50 or more times a second as it hovers in the air.** The tiny bee hummingbird may beat its wings at an amazing 200 times a second. When hovering, the hummingbird holds its body upright and beats its wings backwards and forwards, not up and down, to keep itself in one place in the air. The fast-beating wings make a low buzzing or humming sound that gives these birds their name.

FEED THE BIRDS!

In winter, food can be scarce for birds. You can make your own food cake to help them.

You will need:
225g of suet, lard or dripping
500g of seeds, nuts, biscuit crumbs, cake and other scraps

Ask an adult for help. First melt the fat, and mix it thoroughly with the seed and scraps. Pour it into an old yogurt pot or similar container, and leave it to cool and harden. Remove the cake from the container. Make a hole through the cake, put a string through the hole and hang it from a tree outside.

317 The swift spends nearly all its life in the air and rarely comes to land. It can catch prey, eat, drink and mate on the wing. After leaving its nest, a young swift may not come to land again for two years, and may fly as far as 500,000 kilometres.

Swifts eat insects that they chase and catch in mid-air!

◀ The spine-tailed swift is thought to fly at speeds of up to 160 kilometres an hour.

Swifts have long, slim wings that are perfect for their life in the air

318 The greater roadrunner is a fast mover on land. It runs at speeds of 20 kilometres an hour as it hunts for insects, lizards and birds' eggs to eat. It can fly but seems generally to prefer running.

Superb swimmers

319 Penguins are the best swimmers and divers in the bird world. They live in and around the Antarctic, which is right at the very south of the world. They spend most of their lives in water, where they catch fish and tiny animals called krill to eat, but they do come to land to breed. Their wings act as strong flippers to push them through the water, and their tail and webbed feet help them steer. Penguins sometimes get around on land by tobogganing over ice on their tummies!

Emperor penguin

320 The gentoo penguin is one of the fastest swimming birds. It can swim at up to 27 kilometres an hour – that's faster than most people can run! Mostly, though, penguins probably swim at about 5 to 10 kilometres an hour.

321 The gannet makes an amazing dive from a height of 30 metres above the sea to catch fish in the sea. This seabird spots its prey as it soars above the ocean. Then with wings swept back and neck and beak held straight out in front, the gannet plunges like a dive-bomber. It enters the water, seizes its prey and surfaces a few seconds later.

QUIZ

1. From how high does a gannet dive?
2. How many kinds of penguin are there?
3. How fast can a gentoo penguin swim?
4. How long can an emperor penguin stay underwater?
5. Where do most kinds of penguin live?

Answers:
1. 30 metres
2. 18 3. 27 kilometres an hour
4. 18 minutes 5. Antarctica

Northern gannet

▼ King penguins and emperor penguins regularly dive deeper than 250 metres. Emperor penguins have been timed making dives lasting more than 18 minutes.

King penguin

◄ There are about 18 different kinds of penguin. Most live in and around Antarctica.

143

Looking good!

322 **At the start of the breeding season male birds try to attract females.** Some do this by showing off their beautiful feathers. Others perform special displays or dances. The male peacock has a long train of colourful feathers. When female birds come near, he begins to spread his tail, showing off the beautiful eye-like markings. He dances up and down and shivers the feathers to get the females' attention.

323 **The male bowerbird attracts a mate by making a structure of twigs called a bower.** The bird spends many hours making it attractive, by decorating it with berries and flowers. Females choose the males with the prettiest bowers. After mating, the female goes away and makes a nest for her eggs. The male's bower is no longer needed.

324 **The male roller performs a special display flight to impress his mate.** Starting high in the air, he tumbles and rolls down to the ground while the female watches from a perch. Rollers are brightly coloured insect-eating birds that live in Africa, Europe, Asia and Australia.

Spotted bowerbird

Fawn breasted bowerbird

Black faced golden bowerbird

◀ Bowerbirds live in Australia and New Guinea.

▼ Female peacocks tend to choose the males with the most attractive feathers.

I DON'T BELIEVE IT!

Water birds called great crested grebes perform a courtship dance together. During the dance they offer each other gifts – beakfuls of water weed!

Cocks-of-the-rock

325
The blue bird of paradise hangs upside-down to show off his wonderful feathers. As he hangs, his tail feathers spread out and he swings backwards and forwards while making a special call to attract the attention of female birds. Most birds of paradise live in New Guinea. All the males have beautiful plumage, but females are much plainer.

326
Male cocks-of-the-rock dance to attract mates. Some of the most brightly coloured birds in the world, they gather in groups and leap up and down to show off their plumage to admiring females. They live in the South American rainforest.

327
The nightingale sings its tuneful song to attract females. Courtship is the main reason why birds sing, although some may sing at other times of year. A female nightingale chooses a male for his song rather than his looks.

Night birds

328 Some birds, such as the poorwill, hunt insects at night when there is less competition for prey. The poorwill sleeps during the day and wakes up at dusk to start hunting. As it flies, it opens its beak very wide and snaps moths out of the air.

▲ As well as moths, the poorwill also catches grasshoppers and beetles on the ground.

329 The kakapo is the only parrot that is active at night. It is also a ground-living bird. All other parrots are daytime birds that live in and around trees. During the day the kakapo sleeps in a burrow or under a rock, and at night it comes out to find fruit, berries and leaves to eat. It cannot fly, but it can climb up into trees using its beak and feet. The kakapo only lives in New Zealand.

Kakapo

330 The barn owl is perfectly adapted for night-time hunting. Its eyes are very large and sensitive to the dimmest light. Its ears can pinpoint the tiniest sound and help it to locate prey. Most feathers make a sound as they cut through the air, but the fluffy edges of the owl's feathers soften the sound of wing beats so the owl can swoop silently on its prey.

331

Like bats, the oilbird uses sounds to help it fly in darkness.
As it flies, it makes clicking noises which bounce off objects in the caves in South America where it lives, and help the bird find its way. At night, the oilbird leaves its cave to feed on the fruits of palm trees.

332

Unlike most birds, the kiwi has a good sense of smell which helps it find food at night. Using the nostrils at the tip of its long beak, the kiwi sniffs out worms and other creatures hiding in the soil. It plunges its beak into the ground to reach its prey.

Kiwi

QUIZ

1. Where are the kiwi's nostrils?
2. Where does the kakapo live?
3. What does the oilbird eat?
4. What's special about the barn owl's feathers?
5. What kind of bird is a poorwill?

Answers:
1. At the end of its beak
2. New Zealand 3. The fruits of palm trees 4. They have fluffy edges
5. It is a type of nightjar

Home sweet home

333 Birds make nests in which to lay their eggs and keep them safe. The bald eagle makes one of the biggest nests of any bird. The nest is made of sticks and is built in a tall tree or on rocks. It is used year after year. It can grow as large as 2.5 metres across and 3.5 metres deep – big enough for several people to get into!

334 The female hornbill lays her eggs in prison! The male hornbill walls up his mate and her eggs in a tree hole. He blocks the entrance to the hole with mud, leaving only a small opening. The female looks after the eggs and the male brings food, passing it through the opening. Once the eggs hatch the female has to remain safely in the hole with her young for a few weeks while the male supplies food.

▲ The bald eagle lives in North America. In 1782 the United States adopted the bald eagle as its national bird.

335

The male weaver bird makes a nest from grass and stems. He knots and weaves the pieces together to make a long nest, which hangs from the branch of a tree. The nest makes a warm, cosy home for the eggs and young, and is also very hard for any predator to get into.

1. The male weaver bird twists strips of leaves around a branch or twig.

2. Then, he makes a roof, and an entrance so he can get inside!

3. When it's finished, the long entrance helps to provide a safe shelter for the eggs.

336

The cave swiftlet makes a nest from its own saliva or spit. It uses the spit as glue to make a cup-shaped nest of feathers and grass.

337

The mallee fowl makes a temperature-controlled nest mound. It is made of plants covered with sand. As the plants rot, the inside of the mound gets warmer. The female bird lays her eggs in holes made in the sides of the mound. The male bird then keeps a check on the temperature with his beak. If the mound cools, he adds more sand. If it gets too hot he makes some openings to let warmth out.

Mallee fowl

338

The cuckoo doesn't make a nest at all – she lays her eggs in the nests of other birds! She lays up to 12 eggs, all in different nests. The owner of the nest is called the host bird. The female cuckoo removes one of the host bird's eggs before she puts one of her own in, so the number in the nest remains the same.

I DON'T BELIEVE IT!

Most birds take several minutes to lay an egg. The cuckoo can lay her egg in nine seconds! This allows her to pop her egg into a nest while the owner's back is turned.

Great travellers

339 **The Canada goose spends the summer in the Arctic and flies south in winter.** This regular journey is called a migration. In summer, the Arctic bursts into bloom and there are plenty of plants for the geese to eat while they lay their eggs and rear their young. In autumn, when the weather turns cold, they migrate, this means they leave to fly to warmer climates farther south. This means that the bird gets warmer weather all year round.

▼ The Canada goose tends to return to its birthplace to breed.

▶ The Arctic tern travels farther than any other bird and sees more hours of daylight each year than any other creature.

340 **The Arctic tern makes one of the longest migrations of any bird.** It breeds in the Arctic during the northern summer. Then, as the northern winter approaches, the tern makes the long journey south to the Antarctic – a trip of some 15,000 kilometres – where it catches the southern summer. In this way the tern gets the benefit of long daylight hours for feeding all year round.

◀ The American golden plover is camouflaged in the tundra vegetation by the spectacular patterns on its back.

341

Every autumn, the American golden plover flies up to 12,800 kilometres from North to South America. It breeds on the North American tundra where it feasts on the insects that fill the air during the brief Arctic summer. When summer is over the plover flies to South America for the winter. This means it has plentiful food supplies all year round.

WHO GOES WHERE?

On this world map are the migration routes of the Canada goose, the Arctic tern and the American golden plover. Each one is a different colour. Can you work out which is which?

Answers:
Yellow: Canada goose
Red: Arctic tern
Green: American golden plover

Desert dwellers

342 **Many desert birds have sandy-brown feathers to blend with their surroundings.** This helps them hide from their enemies. The cream-coloured courser lives in desert lands in Africa and parts of Asia. It is hard to see on the ground, but when it flies, the black and white pattern on its wings makes it more obvious. So the courser runs around rather than fly. It feeds on insects and other creatures it digs from the desert sands.

▶ The elf owl is able to catch prey in its feet as it flies.

Cream-coloured courser

343 **Birds may have to travel long distances to find water in the desert.** But this is not always possible for little chicks. To solve this problem, the male sandgrouse has special feathers on his tummy which act like sponges to hold water. He flies off to find water and thoroughly soaks his feathers. He then returns home where his young thirstily gulp down the water that he's brought.

344 **The elf owl makes its nest in a hole in a desert cactus.** This prickly, uncomfortable home helps to keep the owl's eggs safe from enemies, who do not want to struggle through the cactus' spines. The elf owl is one of the smallest owls in the world and is only about 14 centimetres long. It lives in desert areas in the southwest of the USA.

▶ The sandgrouse lives throughout Asia, often in semi-desert areas.

345
The cactus wren eats cactus fruits and berries. This little bird hops about among the spines of cactus plants and takes any juicy morsels it can find. It also catches insects, small lizards and frogs on the ground. Cactus wrens live in the southwestern USA.

I DON'T BELIEVE IT!

The lammergeier vulture drops bones onto rocks to smash them into pieces. It then swallows the soft marrow and even splinters of bone, bit by bit. Powerful acids in the bird's stomach allow the bone to be digested.

346
The lappet-faced vulture scavenges for its food. It glides over the deserts of Africa and the Middle East, searching for dead animals or the left-overs of hunters such as lions. When it spots something, the vulture swoops down and attacks the carcass with its strong hooked bill. Its head and neck are bare so it does not have to spend time cleaning its feathers after feeding from a messy carcass.

▼ The lappet-faced vulture has very broad wings. These are ideal for soaring high above the plains of its African home, searching for food.

Staying safe

347 Birds have clever ways of hiding themselves from enemies. The tawny frogmouth is an Australian bird that hunts at night. During the day, it rests in a tree where its brownish, mottled feathers make it hard to see. If the bird senses danger it stretches itself, with its beak pointing upwards, so that it looks almost exactly like an old broken branch or tree stump.

Tawny frogmouth

348 If a predator comes too close to her nest and young, the female killdeer leads the enemy away by a clever trick. She moves away from the nest, which is made on the ground, making sure the predator has noticed her. She then starts to drag one wing as though she is injured and is easy prey. When she has led the predator far enough away from her young she suddenly flies up into the air and escapes.

▶ The killdeer lives in North America.

349 Guillemots find that there is safety in numbers. Thousands of these birds live together on cliff tops and rocks. They do not build nests but simply lay their eggs on the rock or bare earth. Most land hunters cannot reach the birds on these rocks, and any flying egg thieves are soon driven away by the mass of screeching, pecking birds.

I DON'T BELIEVE IT!

The guillemot's egg is pear-shaped with one end much more pointed than the other. This means that the egg rolls round in a circle if it is pushed or knocked, so does not fall off the cliff.

Safe and sound

350 **A bird's egg protects the developing chick inside.** The yellow yolk in the egg provides the baby bird with food while it is growing. Layers of egg white, called albumen, cushion the chick and keep it warm, while the hard shell keeps everything safe. The shell is porous – it allows air in and out so that the chick can breathe. The parent birds keep the egg warm in a nest. This is called incubation.

1. The chick starts to chip away at the egg.

353 **The kiwi lays an egg a quarter of her own size.** The egg weighs 420 grams – the kiwi only weighs 1.7 kilograms. This is like a new baby weighing 17.5 kilograms, most weigh about 3.5 kilograms.

351 **The biggest egg in the world is laid by the ostrich.** An ostrich egg weighs about 1.5 kilograms – an average hen's egg weighs only about 50 grams. The shell of the ostrich egg is very strong, measuring up to 2 millimetres thick.

352 **The smallest egg in the world is laid by the bee hummingbird.** It weighs about 0.3 grams. The bird itself weighs only 2 grams.

Ostrich egg

Bee hummingbird egg

4. The chick is able to wriggle free. Its parents will look after it for several weeks until it can look after itself.

2. The chick uses its egg tooth to break free.

3. The egg splits wide open.

354

The number of eggs laid in a clutch varies from 1 to more than 20. A clutch is the name for the number of eggs that a bird lays in one go. The number of clutches per year also changes from bird to bird. The grey partridge lays one of the biggest clutches, with an average of 15 to 19 eggs, and the common turkey usually lays 10 to 15 eggs. The emperor penguin lays one egg a year.

QUIZ

1. How thick is the shell of an ostrich egg?
2. How many eggs a year does the emperor penguin lay?
3. How much does the bee hummingbird's egg weigh?
4. For how long does the wandering albatross incubate its eggs?
5. For how long does the great spotted woodpecker incubate its eggs?

Answers:
1. 2 millimetres 2. One 3. 0.3 grams 4. Up to 82 days 5. 10 days

Common turkey

355

The great spotted woodpecker incubates its egg for only 10 days. This is one of the shortest incubation periods of any bird. The longest incubation period is of the wandering albatross, which incubates its eggs for up to 82 days.

Deadly hunters

356 **The golden eagle is one of the fiercest hunters of all birds.** The eagle has extremely keen eyesight and can see objects from a far greater distance than humans can manage. When it spies a victim, the eagle dives down and seizes its prey in its powerful talons. It then rips the flesh apart with its strong hooked beak. The golden eagle usually has two eggs. However, the first chick to hatch often kills the younger chick. Golden eagles live in North America, Europe, North Africa and Asia.

Steller's sea eagle

357 **The sea eagle feeds on fish that it snatches from the water surface.** The eagle soars over the ocean searching for signs of prey. It swoops down, seizes a fish in its sharp claws and flies off to a rock or cliff to eat its meal. Spikes on the soles of the eagle's feet help it hold onto its slippery prey. Other eagles have special prey, too. The snake eagle feeds mostly on snakes and lizards. It has short, rough-surfaced toes that help it grip its prey.

▼ The golden eagle can soar for hours on its huge wings, searching for prey such as rabbits and other birds.

I DON'T BELIEVE IT!

Eagles like to make their nests in high places. One pair of sea eagles made their nest on top of a tall navigation beacon on the coast of Norway.

358 **The raven is the biggest of all the songbirds and a powerful hunter.** It grows up to 63 centimetres long, it has a strong, hooked beak for attacking its victims and it can run fast on the ground as well as fly when chasing prey. Rats and mice are its main catches, but it steals other birds' eggs and can even kill a creature as large as a rabbit. Ravens also scavenge for food, taking animals that are already dead or the remains of the kills of other hunters.

▶ Ravens live in North America, Europe, and parts of Africa and Asia.

Caring for the young

359 Emperor penguins have the worst breeding conditions of any bird. They lay eggs and rear their young on the Antarctic ice. The female penguin lays one egg at the start of the Antarctic winter. She returns to the sea, leaving her partner to incubate the egg on his feet. The egg is covered by a flap of the father's skin and feathers – so it is much warmer than the surroundings.

▲ While the male penguin incubates the egg he does not eat. When the chick hatches, the female returns to take over its care while the exhausted, hungry male finds food.

360 Pigeons feed their young on 'pigeon milk'. This special liquid is made in the lining of part of the bird's throat, called the crop. The young birds are fed on this for the first few days of their life and then start to eat seeds and other solid food.

361 Hawks and falcons care for their young and bring them food for many weeks. Their chicks are born blind and helpless. They are totally dependent on their parents for food and protection until they grow large enough to hunt for themselves.

▶ A sparrowhawk and her chicks.

A mallard, a type of duck, with her ducklings

362
Other birds, such as ducks and geese, are able to run around and find food as soon as they hatch. Baby ducks follow the first moving thing they see when they hatch – usually their mother. This reaction is called imprinting. It is a form of very rapid learning that can happen only in the first few hours of an animal's life. Imprinting ensures that the young birds stay close to their mother and do not wander away.

I DON'T BELIEVE IT!
While male penguins incubate their eggs they huddle together for warmth. The birds take it in turns to stand on the outside and take the force of the freezing winds.

363
Swans carry their young on their back as they swim. This allows the parent bird to move fast without having to wait for the young, called cygnets, to keep up. When the cygnets are riding on the parent bird's back they are safe from enemies.

364
Young birds must learn their songs from adults. A young bird such as a chaffinch is born being able to make sounds. But, like a human baby learning to speak, it has to learn the chaffinch song by listening to its parents and practising.

Deep in the jungle

Harpy eagle

365 **Birds of paradise are among the most colourful of all rainforest birds.** Only the males have brilliant plumage and decorative feathers; the females are generally much plainer. There are about 42 different kinds of birds of paradise and they all live in the rainforests of New Guinea and northeast Australia. Fruit is their main food but some also feed on insects and spiders.

Hoatzin

366 **The Congo peafowl was only discovered in 1936.** It lives in the dense rainforest of West Africa and has rarely been seen. The male bird has beautiful glossy feathers while the female is mostly brown and black.

Congo peafowl

367 **The harpy eagle is the world's largest eagle.** It is about 90 centimetres long and has huge feet and long sharp claws. It feeds on rainforest animals such as monkeys and sloths, which it catches in the trees.

368 **The hoatzin builds its nest overhanging water.** If its chicks are in danger they can escape by dropping into the water and swimming to safety. This strange bird with its ragged crest lives in the Amazon rainforest in South America.

369 **The quetzal has magnificent tail feathers which are up to 90 centimetres long.** This beautiful bird lives in the rainforests of Central America. It was worshipped as a sacred bird by the ancient Mayan and Aztec people.

Quetzal

QUIZ

1. When was the Congo peafowl discovered?
2. How long are the quetzal's tail feathers?
3. How many kinds of birds of paradise are there?
4. Where does the scarlet macaw live?
5. How do the hoatzin's chicks escape danger?

Answers:
1. 1936 2. About 90 centimetres 3. About 42 4. South America 5. They drop out of their nest into the water

370 **The scarlet macaw is one of the largest parrots in the world.** This spectacular bird is 85 centimetres long, including its very long tail and lives in the South American rainforest. It moves in flocks of 20 or so that screech loudly as they fly from tree to tree feeding on fruit and leaves.

Scarlet macaw

371 **The junglefowl is the ancestor of the farmyard chicken.** This colourful bird lives in the Southeast Asian rainforest, where it feeds on seeds and insects.

Junglefowl

The biggest birds

372 The fast-running emu is the largest bird in Australia. Like the ostrich it cannot fly, but it can run at speeds of more than 50 kilometres an hour on its long legs as it searches for fruit, berries and insects to eat. In the breeding season the female lays up to 10 eggs in a dip in the ground. The male then takes over and incubates the clutch.

▼ These flightless birds are among the largest birds in the world.

Emu

Kiwi

▼ The ostrich is the world's fastest two-legged runner. It is specially adapted for speed, and can run at up to 70 kilometres an hour.

Very powerful upper leg muscles

Extra flexible knees

Long, strong legs

Bendy two-toed feet

373 The rhea lives on the grassy plains of South America. It is a fast-running bird but it cannot fly. It eats mainly grass and other small plants, but it also catches insects and other small creatures such as lizards. In the breeding season, male rheas fight to gather a flock of females. Once he has his flock, the male rhea digs a nest in the ground. Each of the females lays her eggs in this nest. The male incubates the eggs, and he looks after the chicks until they are about six months old.

▼ The rhea can sprint faster than a horse, reaching speeds of up to 50 kilometres an hour.

Cassowary

374 Cassowaries are flightless birds which live in the rainforests of Australia and New Guinea. There are three species – all are large birds with long, strong legs and big, sharp-clawed feet. On the cassowary's head is a large horny crest, called a casque. Experts think that when the bird is moving through the dense forest, it holds its head down and uses the casque to help it break its way through the tangle of plants.

I DON'T BELIEVE IT!

One rhea egg is the equivalent to about 12 hen's eggs. It has long been a tasty feast for local people.

Messing about in the river

375 **The jacana can walk on water!** It has amazingly long toes that spread the bird's weight over a large area and allow it to walk on floating lily pads as it hunts for food such as insects and seeds. Jacanas can also swim and dive. There are eight different types of jacana, also called lilytrotters. They live in parts of North and South America, Africa and Asia.

376 **The kingfisher makes its nest in a tunnel in a riverbank.** Using their strong beaks, a male and female pair dig a tunnel up to 60 centimetres long and make a nesting chamber at the end. The female lays up to eight eggs which both parents take turns to look after.

377 **The heron catches fish and other water creatures.** This long-legged bird stands on the shore or in shallow water and reaches forward to grab its prey with a swift thrust of its dagger-like beak.

378 **A small bird called the dipper is well-adapted to river life.** It usually lives around fast-flowing streams and can swim and dive well. It can even walk along the bottom of a stream, snapping up prey such as insects and other small creatures. There are five different types of dipper and they live in North and South America, Asia and Europe.

QUIZ

1. How long is a kingfisher's nest burrow?
2. How many types of jacana are there?
3. What is the osprey's prey?
4. What helps the osprey hold onto its prey?
5. What do pelicans eat?

Answers:
1. About 60 centimetres 2. Eight 3. Fish 4. Spikes on the soles of its feet 5. Fish

379 **The pelican collects fish in the big pouch that hangs beneath its long beak.** When the pelican pushes its beak into the water the pouch stretches and fills with water – and fish. When the pelican then lifts its head up, the water drains out of the pouch leaving any food behind.

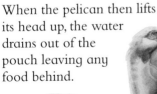

The pelican uses its pouch like a net to catch fish.

380 **The osprey is a bird of prey which feeds mainly on fish.** This bird is found nearly all over the world near rivers and lakes. It watches for prey from the air then plunges into the water with its feet held out in front ready to grab a fish. Special spikes on the soles of its feet help it hold onto its slippery catch.

Can I have some more?

381 **The woodpecker uses its special strong beak to bore into tree trunks and catch insects.** The bird holds on tightly to a tree trunk with the help of its strong feet and sharp claws. Its stiff tail feathers also help to give it support. It starts to hammer into the trunk, disturbing wood-boring insects that live beneath the tree bark. The insects try to flee, but the woodpecker quickly snaps them up.

▶ There are more than 200 different kinds of woodpecker, including this Eurasian woodpecker. They live in North and South America, Africa, Europe and Asia.

382
The antbird keeps watch over army ants as they march through the forest. The bird flies just ahead of the ants and perches on a low branch. It then pounces on the many insects, spiders and other small creatures that try to escape from the marching column of ants. Some antbirds also eat the ants themselves. There are about 240 different types of antbirds that live in Central and South America.

▼ Honeyguides have been known to lead honey-loving humans to bees' nests.

384
The honeyguide bird uses the honey badger to help it get food. The honeyguide feeds on bee grubs and honey. It can find the bees' nests but it is not strong enough to break into them. So it looks for the honey badger to help. It leads the badger toward the bees' nest. When the honey badger smashes into the nest, the honeyguide can also eat its fill.

383
The hummingbird feeds on flower nectar. Nectar is a sweet liquid made by flowers to attract pollinating insects. It is not always easy for birds to reach, but the hummingbird is able to hover in front of the flower while it sips the nectar using its long tongue.

I DON'T BELIEVE IT!

The hummingbird has to eat lots of nectar to get enough energy to survive. If a human were to work as hard as a hummingbird, he or she would need to eat three times their weight in potatoes each day.

Life in snow and ice

385 The coldest places on Earth are the Arctic and the Antarctic. The Arctic is as far north as it is possible to go, and the Antarctic is south, at the bottom of the Earth. The snowy owl is one of the largest birds in the Arctic. Its white feathers hide it in the snow.

386 The snow bunting breeds on Arctic islands and farther north than any other bird. The female makes a nest of grasses, moss and lichens on the ground. She lays four to eight eggs and, when they hatch, both parents help to care for the young. Seeds, buds and insects are the snow bunting's main foods.

387 The ptarmigan has white feathers in the winter to help it hide from enemies among the winter snows in the Arctic. But in summer its white plumage would make it very obvious, so the ptarmigan moults and grows brown and grey feathers.

388 Sheathbills scavenge any food they can find. These large white birds live in the far south on islands close to the Antarctic. They do catch fish but they also search the beaches for any dead animals they can eat. They also snatch weak or dying young from seals and penguins.

Snowy sheathbill

Snowy owl

Snow bunting

Ptarmigan

389
Penguins have a thick layer of fat just under their skin to help protect them from the cold. Their feathers are waterproof and very tightly packed for warmth. Penguins live mainly in Antarctica, but some live in South Africa, South America and Australia.

Emperor penguin

QUIZ

All of these birds live in snow and ice, but some of them live in the north and some live in the south. Can you tell which live in the north, the Arctic, and which live in the south, the Antarctic?

Answers:
All belong in the north, the Arctic, except for the penguins and the snowy sheathbill which belong in the south, the Antarctic.

Tundra swan

390
The tundra swan lays its eggs and rears its young in the tundra of the Arctic. The female bird makes a nest on the ground and lays up to five eggs. Both male and female care for the young. In autumn the whole family migrates, travels south to spend the winter in warmer lands.

Special beaks

391 The snail kite feeds only on water snails and its long upper beak is specially shaped for this strange diet. When the kite catches a snail, it holds it in one foot while standing on a branch or other perch. It strikes the snail's body with its sharp beak and shakes it from the shell.

◄ The snail kite lives in the southern USA, and Central and South America, but it is now very rare.

Toco toucan

393 The wrybill is the only bird with a beak that curves to the right. The wrybill is a type of plover which lives in New Zealand. It sweeps its beak over the ground in circles to pick up insects.

392 The toco toucan's colourful beak is about 19 centimetres long. It allows the toucan to pick fruit and berries at the end of branches that it would not otherwise be able to reach. There are more than 40 different kinds of toucan, and all have large beaks of different colours. The colours and patterns may help the birds attract mates.

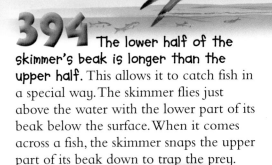

Black skimmer

394 The lower half of the skimmer's beak is longer than the upper half. This allows it to catch fish in a special way. The skimmer flies just above the water with the lower part of its beak below the surface. When it comes across a fish, the skimmer snaps the upper part of its beak down to trap the prey.

I DON'T BELIEVE IT!

The flamingo's legs may look as if they are back to front. In fact, what appear to be the bird's knees are really its ankles!

396 The crossbill has a very unusual beak which crosses at the tip. The shape of this beak allows the bird to open out the scales of pine cones and remove the seeds it feeds on.

395 The flamingo uses its beak to filter food from shallow water. It stands in the water with its head down and its beak beneath the surface. Water flows into the beak and is pushed out again by the flamingo's large tongue. Any tiny creatures such as insects and shellfish are trapped on bristles in the beak.

Birds and people

397 **People buying and selling caged birds has led to some species becoming extremely rare.** Some pet birds such as budgerigars are bred in captivity, but others such as parrots are taken from the wild, even though this is now illegal. The beautiful hyacinth macaw, which used to be common in South American jungles, is now rare because of people stealing them from the wild to sell.

Red-fan parrot

King parrot

Hyacinth macaw

398 **In some parts of the world, people still keep falcons for hunting.** The birds are kept in captivity and trained to kill rabbits and other animals, and bring them back to their master. When the birds are taken out hunting, they wear special hoods over their heads. These are removed when the bird is released to chase its prey.

399 **Many kinds of birds are reared for their eggs and meat.** Chickens and their eggs are a major food in many countries, and ducks, geese and turkeys are also eaten. These are all specially domesticated species but some wild birds, such as pheasants, partridge and grouse, are also used as food.

Starlings

400 Starlings are very common city birds. Huge flocks are often seen gathering to roost, or sleep on buildings. Starlings originally lived in Europe and Asia but have been taken to other countries and been just as successful. For example, 100 years ago 120 starlings were released in New York. Now starlings are among the most common birds in North America. The starling is very adaptable. It will eat a wide range of foods including, insects, seeds and fruits, and will nest almost anywhere.

I DON'T BELIEVE IT!

In one city crows wait by traffic lights. When the lights are red they place walnuts in front of the cars. When the lights turn green the cars move over the nuts, breaking the shells. The birds then fly down and pick up the kernels!

What are mammals?

401 **Mammals are warm-blooded animals with a bony skeleton and fur or hair.** Being warm-blooded means that a mammal can keep its body at a constant temperature, even if the weather is very cold. The skeleton supports the body and protects the delicate parts inside, such as the heart, lungs and brain. There is one sort of mammal you know very well, it's you!

African savanna elephant

Eurasian beaver

Meerkat

Eurasian otter

European water vole

Cheetah

Red panda

Greater
fruit bat

Lion

Western
tarsier

Greater
horseshoe
bat

Racoon-dog

The mammal world

402 **There are nearly 4500 different types of mammal.** Most have babies which grow inside the mother's body. While a baby mammal grows, a special organ called a placenta supplies it with food and oxygen from the mother's body. These mammals are called placental mammals.

▼ This echidna is part of a group of mammals called monotremes. They do not give birth to live young – they lay eggs instead.

404 **Not all mammals' young develop inside the mother's body.** Two smaller groups of mammals do things differently. Monotremes, like platypuses and echidnas or spiny anteaters, lay eggs. The platypus lays her eggs in a burrow, but the echidna keeps her single egg in a special dip in her belly until it is ready to hatch.

Duck-billed platypus

403 **Mammal mothers feed their babies on milk from their own bodies.** The baby sucks this milk from teats on special mammary glands, also called udders or breasts, on the mother's body. The milk contains all the food the young animal needs to help it grow.

▲ Olive baboons live in Africa in groups called troops of between 20 and 150 animals.

QUIZ

1. How many types of mammal are there?
2. Which types of mammal lay eggs?
3. How big is a baby kangaroo when it is born?
4. What supplies food and oxygen to a baby mammal in the womb?

Answers:
1. nearly 4500 2. Platypus and echidnas 3. 2 centimetres 4. The placenta

405 **Marsupials give birth to tiny young that finish developing in a pouch.** A baby kangaroo is only 2 centimetres long when it is born. Tiny, blind and hairless, it makes its own way to the safety of its mother's pouch. Once there, it latches onto a teat in the pouch and begins to feed.

▲ The baby kangaroo stays in the pouch for about six months while it grows.

▲ Fallow deer have a good sense of smell, and excellent sight.

406 **Most mammals have good senses of sight, smell and hearing.** Their senses help them watch out for enemies, find food and keep in touch with each other. For many mammals, smell is their most important sense. Plant-eaters such as rabbits and deer sniff the air for signs of danger such as the scent of a predator.

Big and small

407 **The blue whale is the biggest mammal and the largest animal ever known to have lived.** It can measure more than 33.5 metres long – that's as long as seven family cars parked end to end – and weigh up to 190,000 kilograms. It spends all its life in the sea.

▼ Mammal species range from the giant blue whale to tiny shrews and bats. Here you can see the blue whale to scale with the largest land mammals, and a tiny human!

Blue whale:
33.5 metres long

408 **The elephant is the biggest land mammal.** There are three kinds of elephant – the African savanna elephant, the African forest elephant, and the Asian. The African savanna is the biggest, a full-grown male may weigh as much as 7500 kilograms – more than a hundred adult people. It stands about 4 metres high at the shoulder. Elephants may eat more than 300 kilograms of leaves, twigs and fruit each day.

Giraffe:
5.5 metres tall

Human:
1.7 metres tall

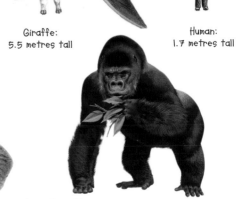

African savanna elephant

409 **Gorillas are the biggest primates.** Primates are the group of mammals to which chimpanzees and humans belong. A full-grown male gorilla is about 1.75 metres tall and weighs as much as 275 kilograms.

410

The giraffe is the tallest of all the mammals. A male giraffe is about 5.5 metres tall – that's more than three or four people standing on each other's shoulders. The giraffe lives in Africa, south of the Sahara desert. Its height helps it reach fresh juicy leaves at the tops of trees.

I DON'T BELIEVE IT!

The African elephant has the biggest nose in the mammal world. A male's nose, or trunk, measures up to 2.5 metres long. Elephants use their trunks for gathering food, fighting and drinking, as well as for smelling.

Brown bear:
2.4 metres tall

African elephant:
4 metres tall

411

The capybara is the largest living rodent. Rodents are the group of mammals that include rats and mice. At about 1.3 metres long the capybara is a giant compared to most rodents. It lives around ponds, lakes and rivers in South America.

412

The smallest mammal in the world is the tiny hog–nosed bat. A full-grown adult's body is only 3 centimetres long. It weighs about 2 grams – less than a teaspoon of rice!

413

The tiny mouse deer is only the size of a hare. Also known as the chevrotain, this little creature is only about 85 centimetres long and stands about 30 centimetres high at the shoulder. It lives in African forests.

Fast movers

414 **The cheetah can run faster than any other animal.** It can move at about 100 kilometres an hour, but it cannot run this fast for long. The cheetah uses its speed to catch other animals to eat. It creeps towards its prey until it is only about 100 metres away. Then it races towards it at top speed, ready for the final attack.

▼ The cheetah's long slender legs and muscular body help it to run fast. The long tail balances the body while it is running.

415 The red kangaroo is a champion jumper. It can leap along at 40 kilometres an hour or more. The kangaroo needs to be able to travel fast. It lives in the dry desert lands of Australia and often has to journey long distances to find grass to eat and water to drink.

▼ The pronghorn is one of the fastest mammals in North America. It has to run to escape its enemies, such as wolves.

▲ The red kangaroo can leap 9 or 10 metres in a single bound.

417 The pronghorn is slower than the cheetah, but it can run for longer. It can keep up a speed of 70 kilometres an hour for about ten minutes.

416 Even the little brown hare can run at more than 70 kilometres an hour. Its powerful back legs help it move fast enough to escape enemies such as foxes.

SPEED DEMONS!

How do you compare to the fastest mammal on earth? Ask an adult to measure how far you can run in 10 seconds. Times this by 6, and then times the answer by 60 to find out how many metres you can run in an hour. If you divide this by 1000 you will get your speed in kilometres per hour. You will find it will be far less than the cheetah's 100 kilometres per hour!

Swimmers and divers

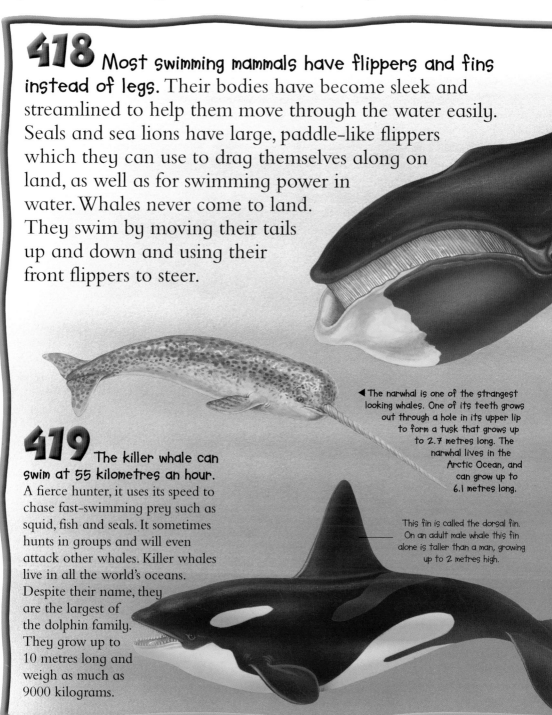

418 **Most swimming mammals have flippers and fins instead of legs.** Their bodies have become sleek and streamlined to help them move through the water easily. Seals and sea lions have large, paddle-like flippers which they can use to drag themselves along on land, as well as for swimming power in water. Whales never come to land. They swim by moving their tails up and down and using their front flippers to steer.

◄ The narwhal is one of the strangest looking whales. One of its teeth grows out through a hole in its upper lip to form a tusk that grows up to 2.7 metres long. The narwhal lives in the Arctic Ocean, and can grow up to 6.1 metres long.

419 **The killer whale can swim at 55 kilometres an hour.** A fierce hunter, it uses its speed to chase fast-swimming prey such as squid, fish and seals. It sometimes hunts in groups and will even attack other whales. Killer whales live in all the world's oceans. Despite their name, they are the largest of the dolphin family. They grow up to 10 metres long and weigh as much as 9000 kilograms.

This fin is called the dorsal fin. On an adult male whale this fin alone is taller than a man, growing up to 2 metres high.

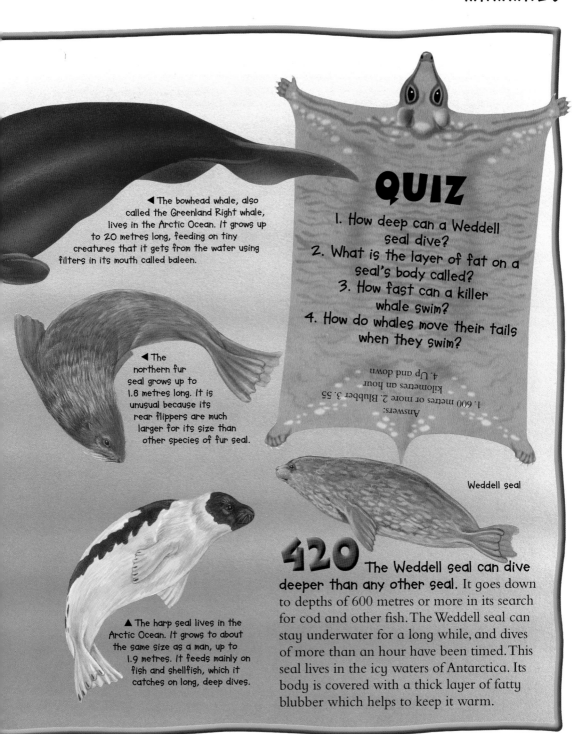

◀ The bowhead whale, also called the Greenland Right whale, lives in the Arctic Ocean. It grows up to 20 metres long, feeding on tiny creatures that it gets from the water using filters in its mouth called baleen.

QUIZ

1. How deep can a Weddell seal dive?
2. What is the layer of fat on a seal's body called?
3. How fast can a killer whale swim?
4. How do whales move their tails when they swim?

Answers:
1. 600 metres or more 2. Blubber 3. 55 kilometres an hour 4. Up and down

◀ The northern fur seal grows up to 1.8 metres long. It is unusual because its rear flippers are much larger for its size than other species of fur seal.

Weddell seal

▲ The harp seal lives in the Arctic Ocean. It grows to about the same size as a man, up to 1.9 metres. It feeds mainly on fish and shellfish, which it catches on long, deep dives.

420 The Weddell seal can dive deeper than any other seal. It goes down to depths of 600 metres or more in its search for cod and other fish. The Weddell seal can stay underwater for a long while, and dives of more than an hour have been timed. This seal lives in the icy waters of Antarctica. Its body is covered with a thick layer of fatty blubber which helps to keep it warm.

Fliers and gliders

421 **Bats are the only true flying mammals.** They zoom through the air on wings made of skin. These are attached to the sides of their body and supported by specially adapted, extra-long bones of the arms and hands. Bats generally hunt at night. During the day they hang upside down by their feet from a branch or cave ledge. Their wings are neatly folded at their sides or around their body.

▲ Fruit-eating bats, such as flying foxes, live in the tropics. They feed mostly on fruit and leaves.

422 **There are more than 950 different types of bat.** They live in most parts of the world, but not in colder areas. Bats feed on many different sorts of food. Most common are the insect-eating bats which snatch their prey from the air while in flight. Others feast on pollen and nectar from flowers. Flesh-eating bats catch fish, birds, lizards and frogs.

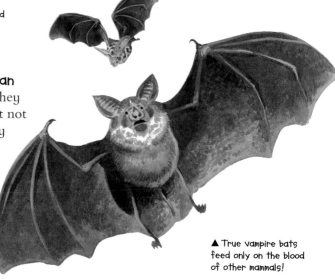

▲ True vampire bats feed only on the blood of other mammals!

423 Flying lemurs don't really fly – they just glide from tree to tree. They can glide distances of up to 130 metres with the help of flaps of skin at the sides of the body. When the flying lemur takes off from a branch it holds its limbs out, stretching the skin flaps so that they act like a parachute.

424 Other gliding mammals are the flying squirrels and gliders. All can glide from tree to tree, like the flying lemur, with the help of flaps of skin at the sides of the body. Flying squirrels live in North America and parts of Asia. Gliders are a type of possum and live in Australia and New Guinea.

I DON'T BELIEVE IT!

A vampire bat consumes about 26 litres of blood a year. That's about as much as the total blood supply of five human beings!

Life in snow and ice

425 The polar bear is the biggest land-based predator in the Arctic. It can run fast, swim well and even dives under the ice to hunt its main prey – ringed seals. It also catches seabirds and land animals such as the Arctic hare and reindeer. The polar bear's thick white fur helps to keep it warm – even the soles of its feet are furry.

426 The musk ox has a long shaggy outer coat to help it survive the arctic cold. A thick undercoat keeps out the damp. The musk ox eats grass, moss and lichen. In winter it digs through the snow with its hooves to reach its food.

427 Caribou, also known as reindeer, feed in arctic lands. The land around the Arctic Ocean is called the tundra. In the short summer plenty of plants grow, the caribou eat their fill and give birth to their young. When summer is over the caribou trek up to 1000 kilometres south to spend the winter in forests.

428
The lemming builds its nest under the snow in winter. The nest is made on the ground from dry plants and twigs. The lemming makes tunnels under the snow from its nest to find grass, berries and lichen to eat. During the summer the lemming nests underground.

I DON'T BELIEVE IT!

Lemmings are very fast breeders. Females can become pregnant at only 14 days old, and they can produce litters of as many as 12 young every month.

429
The walrus uses its long tusks for many tasks. They are used to drag itself out of water and onto the ice as well as for defending itself against enemies and rival walruses. The tusks can grow as much as one metre long.

Walrus

430
The leopard seal is the fiercest hunter in the Antarctic. It lives in the waters around Antarctica and preys on penguins, fish and even other seals. There are no land mammals in the Antarctic.

431
Some arctic animals such as the Arctic hare and the ermine, or stoat, change colour. In winter these animals have white fur which helps them hide among the snow. In summer, when white fur would make them very easy to spot, their coats turn brown.

189

Creatures of the night

432 Not all mammals are active during the day.
Some sleep during the daylight hours and wake up at night. They are called nocturnal mammals, and there are many reasons for their habits. Bats, for example, hunt at night to avoid competition with daytime hunters, such as eagles and hawks. At night, bats and owls have the skies to themselves.

433 The tarsier's big eyes help it to see in the dark.
This little primate lives in Southeast Asian forests where it hunts insects at night. Its big eyes help it make the most of whatever glimmer of light there is from the moon. Like the bats, it probably finds there is less competition for its insect prey at night.

◀ The western tarsier is only 16 centimetres long, but its huge tail can be up to 27 centimetres long.

▼ Red pandas live in Asia, from the country of Nepal to Myanmar (Burma), and in Southwest China.

434 The red panda is a night feeder.
It curls up in a tree and sleeps during the day, but at night it searches for food such as bamboo shoots, roots, fruit and acorns. It also eats insects, birds' eggs and small animals. In summer, though, red pandas sometimes wake up in the day and climb trees to find fresh leaves to eat.

435 Hyenas come out at night to find food.

During the day they shelter underground. Hyenas are scavengers – this means that they feed mainly on the remains of creatures killed by larger hunters. When a lion has eaten its fill, the hyenas rush in to grab the remains.

436 Bats hunt at night.

Insect feeders, such as the horseshoe bat, manage to find their prey by means of a special kind of animal sonar. The bat makes high-pitched squeaks as it flies. If the waves from these sounds hit an animal, such as a moth, echoes bounce back to the bat. These echoes tell the bat where its prey is.

Large ears hear the echoes

QUIZ

1. What do we call animals that come out only at night?
2. Where does the tarsier live?
3. What is a scavenger?
4. How does the horseshoe bat find its prey?
5. What does the red panda eat?

Answers:
1. Nocturnal 2. Southeast Asia 3. An animal that eats the remains of creatures killed by larger hunters 4. By animal sonar 5. Bamboo shoots, fruit, acorns, insects, birds' eggs

Busy builders

437 Beavers start their home building by damming a stream with branches, stones and mud. They do this to make a deep, quiet lake where they can make a winter food store and a shelter called a lodge. Once the dam is made they begin to build the lodge, usually a dome-shaped structure made of sticks and mud. In summer, beavers feed on twigs, leaves and roots. They also collect extra branches and logs to store for the winter.

The beaver gnaws the tree to fell it and eat the soft bark

The entrance to the lodge is usually underwater but the single chamber inside is above water level

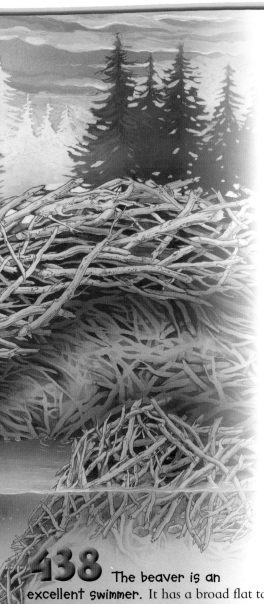

READING MAMMALS!

You can make your own mammal bookmark! Ask an adult to help you cut a piece of white card about 4 centimetres wide by 15 centimetres long. Draw a picture of a mammal onto your piece of card and colour it in. Now you have a mammal to help you read!

439 **The harvest mouse makes a nest on grass stems.** It winds some strong stems round one another to make a kind of platform. She then weaves some softer grass stems into the structure to form a ball–like shape about 10 centimetres across.

438 **The beaver is an excellent swimmer.** It has a broad flat tail, which acts like a paddle when swimming, and it has webbed feet. It dives well, too, and can stay underwater for five minutes or more. To warn others of danger, a beaver may slap the water with its tail as it dives.

Family life

440 **Many mammals live alone, except when they have young, but others live in groups.** Wolves live in family groups called packs. The pack is led by an adult female and her mate and may include up to 20 other animals.

441 **Chimpanzees live in troops of anything from 15 to 80 animals.** There are different types of troops, some are all male, some are just females with young, and some have males, females and young, led by an adult male. Each troop has its own territory which varies in size depending on how many animals are in the troop, and how far they need to travel for food. Troop bonds are loose and animals often move from one to another.

442 **Lions live in groups called prides.** The pride may include one or more adult males, females related to each other, and their young. The average number in a pride is 15. Female young generally stay with the pride of their birth but males must leave before they are full-grown. Lions are unusual in their family lifestyle – all other big cats live alone.

443

A type of mongoose called a meerkat lives in large groups of up to 30 animals. The group is called a colony and contains several family units of a pair of adults along with their young. The colony lives in a network of underground burrows. The members of the colony guard each other against enemies.

I DON'T BELIEVE IT!

Lions may be fierce but they are also very lazy. They sleep and snooze for more than 20 hours of the day!

444

Naked mole rats live underground in a colony of animals led by one female. The colony includes about 100 animals and the ruling female, or queen, is the only one that produces young. Other colony members live like worker bees – they dig the burrows to find food for the group, and look after the queen.

445

Some whales live in families too. Pilot whales, for example, live in groups of 20 or more animals that swim and hunt together. A group may include several adult males and a number of females and their young.

446

The male elephant seal fights rival males to gather a group of females. This group is called a harem and the male seal defends his females from other males. The group does not stay together for long after mating.

Desert dwellers

447 Many desert animals burrow underground to escape the scorching heat. The North African gerbil, for example, stays hidden all day and comes out at night to find seeds and insects to eat. This gerbil is so well adapted to desert life that it never needs to drink. It gets all the liquid it needs from its food.

North African gerbil

▼ Most camels are kept by people in the desert, but some still live wild.

448 The large ears of the fennec fox help it to lose heat from its body. This fox lives in the North African desert. For its size, it has the largest ears of any dog or fox.

Large ears also give the fennec fox very good hearing

449 A camel can last for weeks without drinking water. It can manage on the liquid it gets from feeding on desert plants. But when it does find some water it drinks as much as 80 litres at one time. It does not store water in its hump, but it can store fat.

450 The bactrian camel has thick fur to keep it warm in winter. It lives in the Gobi Desert in Asia where winter weather can be very cold indeed. In summer, the camel's long shaggy fur drops off, leaving the camel almost hairless.

451

The kangaroo rat never needs to drink. A mammal's kidneys control how much water there is in the animal's body. The kangaroo rat's kidneys are much more efficient than ours. It can even make some of its food into water inside its body!

▶ The kangaroo rat is named because it has long, strong back legs and can jump like a kangaroo.

QUIZ

1. How much water can a camel drink in one go?
2. Where does the bactrian camel live?
3. What dangerous animal does the desert hedgehog eat?
4. Which animals never need to drink?
5. Where does Pallas's cat live?

Answers:
1. 80 litres 2. Gobi Desert
3. Scorpions 4. Kangaroo rat and the North
African gerbil 5. The Gobi Desert

452

The desert hedgehog eats scorpions as well as insects and birds' eggs. It carefully nips off the scorpion's deadly sting before eating.

▲ The desert hedgehog digs a short, simple burrow into the sand. It stays there during the day to escape the heat.

453

Pallas's cat lives in the Gobi Desert. Its fur is thicker and longer than that of any other small cat to keep it warm in the cold Gobi winter. Pallas's cat lives alone, usually in a cave or a burrow and hunts small creatures such as mice and birds.

On the prowl

454 Mammals which hunt and kill other creatures are called carnivores. Examples of carnivores are animals such as lions, tigers, wolves and dogs. Meat is a more concentrated food than plants so many carnivores do not have to hunt every day. One kill will last them for several days.

▶ Most carnivores will hunt creatures smaller than themselves. The tiger can more easily catch and kill smaller prey like this water deer.

455 The tiger is the biggest of the big cats and an expert hunter. It hunts alone, often at night, and buffalo, deer and wild pigs are its usual prey. The tiger cannot run fast for long so it prefers to creep up on its prey without being noticed. Its striped coat helps to keep it hidden among long grasses. When it is as close as possible to its prey, the tiger makes a swift pounce and kills its victim with a bite to the neck. The tiger clamps its powerful jaws around the victim's throat and suffocates it.

456 Bears eat many different sorts of food. They are carnivores but most bears, except for the polar bear, eat more plant material than meat. Brown bears eat fruit, nuts and insects and even catch fish. In summer, when salmon swim up rivers to lay their eggs, the bears wade into the shallows and hook fish from the water with their mighty paws.

MAKE A FOOD CHAIN

Make your own food chain. Draw a picture of a large carnivore such as a lion and tie it to a piece of string. Then draw a picture of an animal that the lion catches such as a zebra. Hang that from the picture of the lion. Lastly draw a picture of lots of grass and plants (the food of the zebra). Hang that from the picture of the zebra.

457 Hunting dogs hunt in packs. Together, they can bring down a much larger animal. The pack sets off after a herd of plant-eaters such as zebras or gazelles. They try to separate one animal that is perhaps weaker or slower from the rest of the herd.

Fighting back

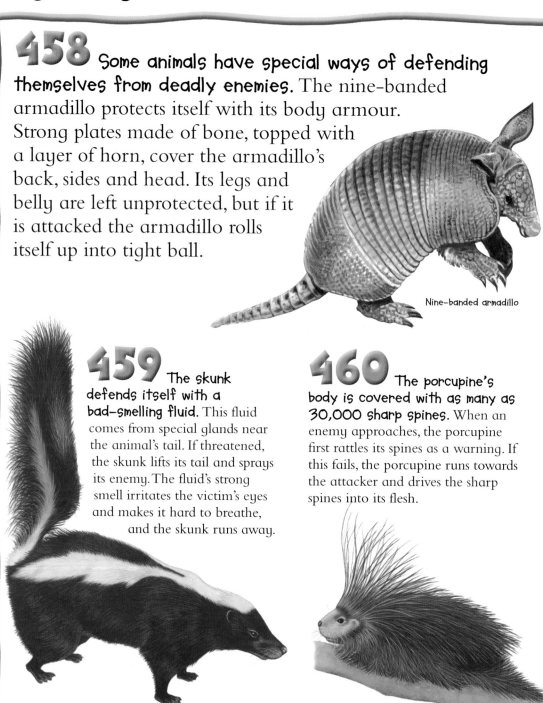

458 **Some animals have special ways of defending themselves from deadly enemies.** The nine-banded armadillo protects itself with its body armour. Strong plates made of bone, topped with a layer of horn, cover the armadillo's back, sides and head. Its legs and belly are left unprotected, but if it is attacked the armadillo rolls itself up into tight ball.

Nine-banded armadillo

459 **The skunk defends itself with a bad-smelling fluid.** This fluid comes from special glands near the animal's tail. If threatened, the skunk lifts its tail and sprays its enemy. The fluid's strong smell irritates the victim's eyes and makes it hard to breathe, and the skunk runs away.

460 **The porcupine's body is covered with as many as 30,000 sharp spines.** When an enemy approaches, the porcupine first rattles its spines as a warning. If this fails, the porcupine runs towards the attacker and drives the sharp spines into its flesh.

461

A rhinoceros may charge its enemies at top speed.

Rhinoceroses are generally peaceful animals but a female will defend her calf fiercely. If the calf is threatened, she will gallop towards the enemy with her head down and lunge with her sharp horns. Few predators will stay around to challenge an angry rhino.

I DON'T BELIEVE IT!
Smelly skunks sometimes feed on bees. They roll the bees on the ground to remove their stings before eating them.

▲ The sight of a full-grown rhinoceros charging is enough to make most predators turn and run.

462

The pangolin's body is protected by tough overlapping scales. These make the animal look rather like a giant pinecone. The pangolin feeds mainly on ants and termites and its thick scales protect it from the stinging bites of its tiny prey.

Deep in the jungle

463 Jungle mammals live at all levels of the forest from the tallest trees to the forest floor. Bats fly over the tree tops and monkeys and apes swing from branch to branch. Lower down, smaller creatures, such as civets and pottos, hide among the dense greenery.

Moustached bat

Angwantibo

Pygmy chimpanzee

Gorilla

Talapoin

Jaguar

Giant armadillo

Civet

464 The jaguar is one of the fiercest hunters in the jungle. It lives in the South American rainforest and is the largest cat in South America. The pig-like peccary and the capybara – a large jungle rodent – are among its favourite prey.

465 The howler monkey has the loudest voice in the jungle. Each troop of howler monkeys has its own special area, called a territory. Males in rival troops shout at each other to defend their territory. Their shouts can be heard from nearly 5 kilometres away.

466 The sloth hardly ever comes down to the ground. This jungle creature lives hanging from a branch by its special hook-like claws. It is so well adapted to this life that its fur grows downwards – the opposite way to that of most mammals – so that rainwater drips off more easily.

Two-toed sloth

I DON'T BELIEVE IT!
The sloth is the slowest animal in the world. In the trees it moves along at only about 5 metres a minute. On the ground it moves even more slowly – about 2 metres a minute!

467 Some monkeys, such as the South American woolly monkey, have a long tail that they use as an extra limb when climbing. This is called a prehensile tail. It contains a powerful system of bones and muscles so it can be used for gripping.

468 Tapirs are plump pig–like animals which live on the jungle floor. There are three different kinds of tapir in the South American rainforests and one kind in the rainforests of Southeast Asia. Tapirs have long bendy snouts and they feed on leaves, buds and grass.

▼ This Brazilian tapir is often found near water and is a good swimmer.

469 The okapi uses its long tongue to pick leaves from forest trees. This tongue is so long that the okapi can lick its own eyes clean! The okapi lives in the African rainforest.

Strange foods

470 **Some mammals only eat one or two kinds of food.** The giant panda, for instance, feeds mainly on the shoots and roots of the bamboo plant. It spends up to 12 hours a day eating, and gobbles up about 12 kilograms of bamboo a day. The panda also eats small amounts of other plants such as irises and crocuses, and very occasionally hunts small creatures such as mice and fish. Giant pandas live in the bamboo forests of central China.

▼ People used to think that vampire bats sucked blood up through fangs. Now we know that they lap like a cat.

▲ There are very few giant pandas left in the world. Their homes are being cut down, which leaves them with nothing to eat.

471 **The vampire bat feeds only on blood – it is the only bat which has this special diet.** The vampire bat hunts at night. It finds a victim such as a horse or cow and crawls up its leg onto its body. The bat shaves away a small area of flesh and, using its long tongue, laps up the blood that flows from the wound. The vampire bat feeds for about 30 minutes, and probably drinks about 26 litres of blood a year.

472

Tiny ants and termites are the main foods of the giant anteater. The anteater breaks open the insects' nests with its strong hooked claws. It laps up huge quantities of the creatures, their eggs and their young with its long tongue. This tongue is about 60 centimetres long and has a sticky surface that helps the anteater to catch the insects.

Giant anteater

473

The mighty blue whale eats only tiny shrimp–like creatures called krill. The whale strains these from the water through a special filter system in its mouth called baleen. It may eat up to 4 tonnes of krill a day.

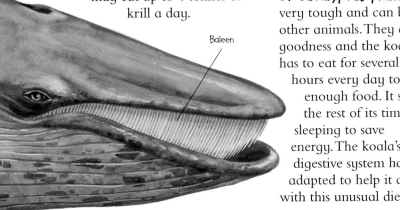

Baleen

474

The koala eats the leaves of eucalyptus plants. These leaves are very tough and can be poisonous to many other animals. They do not contain much goodness and the koala has to eat for several hours every day to get enough food. It spends the rest of its time sleeping to save energy. The koala's digestive system has adapted to help it cope with this unusual diet.

Tool users

475 **The chimpanzee is one of the few mammals to use tools to help it find food.** It uses a stone like a hammer to crack nuts, and uses sticks to pull down fruit from the trees and for fighting. It also uses sticks to help catch insects.

▶ The chimp pokes a sharp stick into a termite or ant nest. It waits a moment or two and then pulls the stick out, covered with juicy insects which it can eat.

▶ Chimps have also discovered that leaves make a useful sponge for soaking up water to drink or for wiping their bodies. Scientists think that baby chimps are not born knowing how to use tools. They have to learn their skills by watching adults at work.

476

The sea otter uses a stone to break open its shellfish food. It feeds mainly on sea creatures with hard shells, such as mussels, clams and crabs. The sea otter lies on its back in the water and places a rock on its chest. It then bangs the shellfish against the rock until the shell breaks, allowing the otter to get at the soft meat inside.

▲ The sea otter spends most of its life in the waters of the North Pacific and is an expert swimmer and diver.

477

The cusimanse is a very clever kind of mongoose. It eats frogs, reptiles, mammals and birds, but it also eats crabs and birds' eggs. When it comes across a meal that is protected by a tough shell, it throws it back between its hind legs against a stone or tree to break it open and get at the tasty insides!

ANIMAL POSTERS

Take a sheet of paper and trace as many predators from this book as you can find. Colour them in and put a big heading — PREDATORS. Take another sheet and trace all the plant-eaters you can find. Put a big heading — PLANT-EATERS.

PREDATORS   PLANT-EATERS

City creatures

478 **Foxes are among the few large mammals which manage to survive in towns and cities.** Once foxes found all their food in the countryside, but now more and more have discovered that city rubbish bins are a good hunting ground. The red fox will eat almost anything. It kills birds, rabbits, eats insects, fruit and berries and takes human leavings.

479 **Raccoons also live in city areas and raid rubbish bins for food.** Like foxes, they eat lots of different kinds of food, including fish, nuts, seeds, berries and insects, as well as what they scavenge from humans. They are usually active at night and spend the day in a den made in a burrow, a hole in rocks or even in the corner of an empty city building.

480 Rats and mice are among the most successful of all mammals. They live all over the world and they eat almost any kind of food. The brown rat and the house mouse are among the most common. The brown rat eats seeds, fruit and grain, but it will also attack birds and mice. In cities it lives in cellars and sewers, anywhere there is rotting food and rubbish. The house mouse hides under floors and in cupboards. It will eat any human food it can find, as well as paper, glue and even soap!

I DON'T BELIEVE IT!

Rats will eat almost anything. They have been known to chew through electrical wires, lead piping and even concrete dams. In the United States rats are said to cause up to 1 billion dollars' worth of damage every year!

Fresh water mammals

481 **Most river mammals spend only part of their time in water.** Creatures such as the river otter and the water rat live on land and go into the water to find food. The hippopotamus, on the other hand, spends most of its day in water to keep cool. Its skin needs to stay moist, and it cracks if it gets too dry.

▶ The hippo is not a good swimmer but it can walk on the riverbed. It can stay underwater for up to half an hour.

482 **Webbed feet make the water rat a good swimmer.** They help the rat push its way through water. Other special features for a life spent partly in water include its streamlined body and small ears.

Water opossum

483 **The water opossum is the only marsupial that lives in water.** Found around lakes and streams in South America, it hides in a burrow during the day and dives into the river at night to find fish.

▼ When a platypus has found its food, it stores it in its cheeks until it has time to eat it.

484 The platypus uses its duck-like beak to find food in the riverbed.

This strange beak is extremely sensitive to touch and to tiny electric currents given off by prey. The platypus dives down to the bottom of the river and digs in the mud for creatures such as worms and shrimps.

Eurasian otter

485 The river otter's ears close off when it is swimming.

This stops water getting into them when the otter dives. Other special features are the otter's webbed feet, and its short, thick fur, which keeps its skin dry.

QUIZ

1. When are city foxes most active?
2. Do raccoons eat only seeds and berries?
3. What are the most common types of rats and mice?
4. Which is the only marsupial that lives in water?
5. What does the platypus eat?
6. Where do river dolphins live?
7. How does the water rat swim?

Answers:
1. At night 2. No, they also eat fish, nuts and insects 3. Brown rats and house mice 4. Water opossum 5. Worms, shrimps and snails 6. Asia and South America 7. With the help of its webbed feet

486 Most dolphins are sea creatures but some live in rivers.

There are five different kinds of river dolphins living in rivers in Asia and South America. All feed on fish and shellfish. They probably use echolocation, a kind of sonar like that used by bats, to find their prey.

▲ The Ganges dolphin is blind but can find food by skillful use of echolocation.

Plant-eaters

487 Plant-eaters must spend much of their time eating in order to get enough nourishment. A zebra spends at least half its day munching grass. The advantage of being a plant-eater, though, is that the animal does not have to chase and compete for its food like hunters do.

▲ Carnivores, such as lions, feed on plant-eaters, so there must always be more plant-eaters than there are carnivores for this 'food chain' to work successfully.

Queensland blossom bat

488 Some kinds of bat feed on pollen and nectar. The Queensland blossom bat, for example, has a long brush-like tongue which it plunges deep into flowers to gather its food. As it feeds it pollinates the flowers – it takes the male pollen to the female parts of a flower so that it can bear seeds and fruits.

489 Rabbits have strong teeth for eating leaves and bark. The large front teeth are called incisors and they are used for biting leaves and chopping twigs. The incisors keep growing throughout the rabbit's life – if they did not they would soon wear out. Farther back in the rabbit's mouth are broad teeth for chewing.

I DON'T BELIEVE IT!

Manatees are said to have been the origin of sailors' stories about mermaids. Short-sighted sailors may have mistaken these plump sea creatures for beautiful women.

490 The manatee is a water-living mammal which feeds on plants. There are three different kinds of these large, gentle creatures: two live in fresh water in West Africa and in the South American rainforest, and the third lives in the west Atlantic, from Florida to the Amazon.

Manatee

Dugong

◄ Manatees, and their relations dugongs, feed on plants such as water weeds, water lilies and seaweeds.

491 Plants are the main foods of most monkeys. Monkeys live in tropical forests where there are plenty of fresh leaves and ripe fruit all year round. Some will also eat insects and other small creatures.

White-cheeked mangabey

Digging deep

492 **Champion burrowers of the mammal world are prairie dogs.** These little animals are not dogs at all but a kind of plump short-tailed squirrel. There are five different species, all of which live in North America. They live in large burrows, which contain several chambers linked by tunnels.

▲ A family of prairie dogs is called a coterie and contains about eight animals – a male, several females and young. A large number of coteries live close to each other in huge colonies, called 'towns', which may cover hundreds of kilometres. Prairie dogs feed on grass and other plants.

493 Moles have specially adapted front feet for digging. The feet are very broad and are turned outward for pushing through the soil. They have large strong claws. The mole has very poor sight. Its sense of touch is very well developed and it has sensitive bristles on its face.

I DON'T BELIEVE IT!

Prairie dogs are not always safe in their own homes. Sometimes burrowing owls move into part of a burrow and then prey on the animals already living there.

European mole

494 Badgers dig a network of chambers and tunnels called a sett. There are special areas in the sett for breeding, sleeping and food stores. Sleeping areas are lined with dry grass and leaves which the badgers sometimes take outside to air for a while.

▼ Badgers usually stay in the burrow during the day and come out at dusk. They are playful creatures and adults are often seen chasing and even leapfrogging with their cubs.

215

Mothers and babies

495 Most whales are born tail first. If the baby emerged head first it could drown during the birth process. As soon as the baby has fully emerged, the mother, with the help of other females, gently pushes it up to the surface to take its first breath. The female whale feeds her baby on milk, just like other mammals.

496 The blue whale has a bigger baby than any other mammal. At birth the baby is about 7 metres long and weighs 2000 kilograms – that's more than 30 average people. It drinks as much as 500 litres of milk a day!

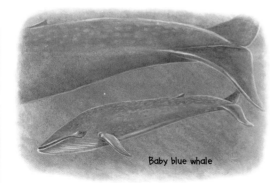

Baby blue whale

497 A baby panda weighs only about 100 grams at birth – that's about as big as a white mouse. It is tiny compared to its mother, who may weigh 100 kilograms or more. The newborn cub is blind and helpless, with a thin covering of white fur. By four weeks it has black and white fur like an adult, and its eyes open when it is two to three months old. It starts to walk when it is about four months and begins to eat bamboo at six months.

498 **Some babies have to be up and running less than an hour after birth.** If the young of animals such as antelopes were as helpless as the baby panda they would immediately be snapped up by predators. They must get to their feet and be able to move with the herd as quickly as possible or they will not survive.

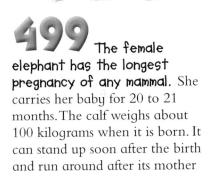

499 **The female elephant has the longest pregnancy of any mammal.** She carries her baby for 20 to 21 months. The calf weighs about 100 kilograms when it is born. It can stand up soon after the birth and run around after its mother when it is a few days old.

Virginia opossum

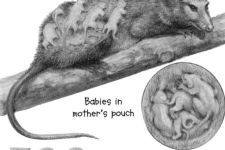

Babies in mother's pouch

500 **The Virginia opossum has as many as 21 babies at one time – more than any other mammal.** The young are only a centimetre long, and all of the babies together weigh only a couple of grams.

Index

Index

Index